Strategies for Achieving Success

33 Life Success Tactics Rooted in the Principles of War

DR JOHN BRACKETT

Contents

INTRODUCTION

In the annals of human history, the principles of war have been studied, analyzed, and perfected through countless battles and conflicts. These principles, ranging from strategy and tactics to leadership and resilience, have often been the defining factors in determining victory or defeat. But what if we could apply these age-old principles not just to the battlefield, but to the battlefield of life itself?
Welcome to a journey of discovery, where we explore how the timeless wisdom derived from the art of war can be harnessed to conquer the challenges we encounter in our daily lives. This book delves into 33 life success tactics that are deeply rooted in the principles of war. These tactics, when adapted and applied to the complexities of modern life, can become powerful tools for achieving our goals, overcoming obstacles, and emerging victorious in our personal and professional endeavors.

Drawing from the experiences of great military leaders, strategists, and warriors throughout history, we'll delve into the strategic mindset required to confront life's trials and tribulations. We'll explore leadership and influence, resilience and perseverance, time management and productivity, conflict resolution and negotiation, personal development, and the strategies needed to thrive in the ever-evolving modern world.

As we embark on this transformative journey, let us remember that the battlefield of life, like any battlefield, requires planning, adaptability, and a well-considered strategy. By embracing the principles of war, we can gain valuable insights, tools, and techniques that will empower us to achieve our aspirations and emerge triumphant in the pursuit of success.

I

The Strategic Mindset

In the grand tapestry of life, the essence of a strategic mindset transcends the boundaries of time and circumstance. It is a quality that has been embraced by both military commanders on the field of battle and visionaries in the boardroom. Part I of our journey delves into the very foundation of this mindset and how it equips us with the tools necessary to navigate the complexities of life successfully.

Embracing the Warrior's Mentality

The warrior's mentality, drawn from the annals of military history, is a mindset that beckons us to adopt unwavering courage, discipline, and a commitment to our chosen path. In this chapter, we explore the qualities of determination, resilience, and the unyielding spirit that defines a warrior. Just as generals lead their troops with unwavering conviction, we too can draw strength from within to face the challenges life presents.

The warrior's mentality goes beyond the battlefield, transcending physical combat to encompass the mental and emotional fortitude needed to conquer the challenges of life. Here, we explore the key facets of this mindset and its relevance to personal development and success.

Embracing the warrior's mentality involves adopting a set of traits and beliefs that enable individuals to confront adversity with strength, resilience, and unwavering determination. While the term "warrior" may evoke images of battle, it is essential to understand that, in the context of personal development, the warrior is a metaphorical representation of someone who faces life's obstacles head-on. Key Elements of the Warrior's Mentality:

Courage: At the core of the warrior's mentality is courage—the ability to confront fear, uncertainty, and challenges with unwavering determination. It involves taking calculated risks and refusing to succumb to self-doubt.

Resilience: Warriors possess resilience, bouncing back from setbacks and adversity with greater strength and determination. They view challenges as opportunities for growth rather than insurmountable obstacles.

Discipline: Discipline is a fundamental component of the warrior's mentality. It involves self-control, adherence to a code of ethics or values, and the ability to stay committed to one's goals and principles.

Adaptability: Warriors are adaptable, capable of adjusting their strategies and approaches as circumstances change. They recognize the need for flexibility and creative problem-solving.

Mental Toughness: A warrior's mentality encompasses mental toughness, which enables individuals to stay focused, maintain a positive attitude, and persevere through adversity.

Mission and Purpose: Warriors have a clear sense of mission or purpose that drives their actions and decisions. They understand their objectives and remain committed to achieving them.

Embracing the warrior's mentality is not without its challenges. It often requires facing discomfort, taking on difficult tasks, and persevering through adversity. However, these challenges lead to personal growth, increased self-confidence, and a greater sense of purpose.

In conclusion, the warrior's mentality is a powerful mindset for personal development and achieving success. It involves embracing courage, resilience, discipline, adaptability, and a strong sense of mission. By adopting this mentality, individuals can tackle life's challenges with strength, determination, and a commitment to their objectives, ultimately fostering personal growth and resilience in the face of adversity.

2

The Power of Vision and Goal Setting

Military campaigns begin with a well-defined objective, and so should our life's endeavors. This introduces the concept of vision and goal setting, revealing how this practice provides a clear direction for our efforts. Like a commander formulates a battle plan, we learn to craft a vision for our lives and set goals that serve as our strategic markers, guiding us towards success.

Vision and goal setting are the twin pillars upon which personal and professional achievements are built. They provide a clear sense of direction and purpose, serving as a roadmap to guide individuals towards their aspirations and dreams. Here, we delve into the profound impact and significance of vision and goal setting in the journey toward success.

A vision is the vivid mental image of a desired future state. It encapsulates what an individual or organization aims to achieve, inspiring action and commitment. The power of vision lies in its ability to:

Provide Clarity: A well-defined vision clarifies the overarching objectives, making it easier to understand where you are heading and what you want to accomplish.

Motivate and Inspire: A compelling vision motivates and inspires people to work towards a common goal. It ignites passion and enthusiasm.

Cultivate Resilience: When challenges arise, a strong vision acts as a source of resilience. It reminds individuals of their ultimate purpose, helping them push through difficulties.

Set the Foundation for Goal Setting: Vision acts as the foundation for setting specific, actionable goals. It provides the "why" behind the goals, making them more meaningful. Goals are the tangible, measurable steps and objectives that align with a vision. Goal setting is a structured process that translates a vision into actionable tasks. The power of goal setting is evident in its ability to:

Create Focus: Setting goals hones your attention on specific tasks and prevents distraction, ensuring you make steady progress towards your vision.

Measure Progress: Goals provide a means to track your advancement. They offer concrete indicators of success and areas that may require adjustments.

Boost Accountability: Clearly defined goals make individuals more accountable for their actions, encouraging commitment and dedication.

Enhance Time Management: Goal setting aids in effective time management by prioritizing tasks that contribute directly to your vision.

Build Confidence: Achieving goals reinforces self-confidence and a sense of accomplishment, motivating you to tackle even greater challenges.

The Symbiotic Relationship: ***Vision and Goal Setting***

The power of vision and goal setting lies in their symbiotic relationship. Vision provides the overarching purpose and direction, while goal setting breaks it down into actionable steps.

While vision and goal setting are powerful tools, they are not without challenges. Overcoming obstacles, setbacks, and unforeseen circumstances is part of the journey. However, it's through these challenges that individuals build resilience, determination, and a greater appreciation for their vision.

In conclusion, the power of vision and goal setting is immeasurable in personal and professional success. Vision provides the inspiration, direction, and purpose, while goal setting transforms it into tangible action steps. This dynamic duo serves as a blueprint for achievement, guiding individuals towards their dreams and aspirations, and empowering them to overcome challenges with unwavering determination.

3

Adaptability and Flexibility: Lessons from Battlefield Strategies

The battlefield is a dynamic and ever-changing environment, demanding adaptability and flexibility from those who engage in it. Similarly, life presents us with unforeseen challenges and opportunities. In this chapter, we uncover valuable lessons from battlefield strategies, demonstrating how an adaptive approach equips us to navigate life's twists and turns with poise and ingenuity. In an ever-evolving world, adaptability and flexibility are essential qualities that empower individuals to navigate uncertainty, embrace change, and excel in a variety of situations. Here, we explore the significance of these attributes and their impact on personal and professional success based on the true view of Adaptability and Flexibility

Adaptability is the capacity to adjust, modify, or evolve in response to changing circumstances or new challenges. It's characterized by the ability to:

Embrace Change: Rather than resisting change, adaptable individuals welcome it as an opportunity for growth and learning.

Learn Quickly: They have a keen ability to grasp new concepts, acquire new skills, and adjust to different environments.

Remain Resilient: Adaptable individuals bounce back from setbacks and continue moving forward, undeterred by obstacles.

Problem-Solve Effectively: They can analyze situations and find innovative solutions to address challenges and seize opportunities.

Thrive in Ambiguity: Adaptability allows individuals to excel even in situations where information is limited or unclear

Flexibility: The Art of Adjusting and Shifting

Flexibility is the capacity to change, adapt, or bend without breaking. It complements adaptability by enabling individuals to:

Modify Plans: Flexible individuals are open to revising their plans and strategies when necessary, recognizing that rigidity can be counterproductive.

Accommodate Others: They can adjust their behavior, communication style, and expectations to collaborate effectively with different people and personalities.

Balance Priorities: Flexibility allows individuals to prioritize tasks and responsibilities based on changing needs and deadlines.

Maintain Work-Life Balance: Being flexible with work hours and personal commitments enables individuals to strike a healthy work–life balance.

Enhance Creativity: A flexible mindset encourages creative thinking and the exploration of diverse solutions to problems.

The Synergy of Adaptability and Flexibility:

Adaptability and flexibility are intertwined and work in harmony:

Adaptability allows individuals to thrive in changing environments and remain agile in the face of shifting circumstances. Flexibility complements adaptability by enabling individuals to adjust their approaches and behaviors as they navigate these changing environments.

Furthermore, they empower individuals to seize opportunities, overcome challenges, and thrive in the face of uncertainty; adaptability and flexibility are indispensable qualities for personal and professional success. They equip individuals with the resilience and versatility needed to excel in a rapidly changing world. By embracing these attributes, individuals can thrive, innovate, and overcome obstacles, turning uncertainty into an opportunity for growth and achievement.

4

Planning and Decision-Making: The Art of Strategy

Just as military commanders meticulously plan their campaigns and make crucial decisions, so too must we craft our life's strategies with care and precision. Chapter 4 delves into the art of strategic planning and decision-making, offering insights into how we can make informed choices that align with our goals and values. Strategy is a methodical and deliberate approach to achieving specific goals or outcomes. It involves a comprehensive plan, often designed to address complex situations or challenges. The art of strategy embodies several key elements: Long-Term

Vision, Resource Allocation, and Competitive Advantage

In Part I, we embark on a journey to cultivate the strategic mindset required to conquer life's challenges. Drawing upon the timeless wisdom of war, we will learn to embrace the warrior's mentality, craft a compelling vision for our lives, adapt to changing circumstances, and make purposeful decisions. Through these teachings, we prepare ourselves for the battles of life, equipping us with the wisdom and strength to achieve success, no matter the terrain.

Planning and decision-making are integral components of personal and professional achievement, guiding individuals and organizations in setting objectives, charting courses, and navigating the complexities of life and business. Here, we explore the pivotal roles of planning and decision-making in the pursuit of success.

Planning is the structured process of defining objectives and outlining the steps necessary to reach those goals. Key attributes of effective planning include:

Goal Clarity: Clear and specific goals provide the foundation for planning. They serve as the destination toward which planning is directed.

Resource Allocation: Effective planning involves allocating resources, including time, finances, and personnel, in a way that optimizes their utility for goal attainment.

Sequencing and Timing: Plans should detail the sequence of actions and the timing of each step to ensure that activities occur in the most logical and efficient order.

Contingency Planning: Effective planning acknowledges that unforeseen challenges may arise. Contingency plans account for these contingencies and outline strategies to address them.

Long-Term Vision: Planning often extends beyond immediate goals and considers long-term objectives, ensuring that actions align with overarching aspirations.

21

II

Leadership and Influence

In the theater of life, the qualities of leadership and influence hold a paramount position. Borrowed from the commanding figures of military history, the principles encapsulated in this section offer an invaluable blueprint for those aspiring to make a mark, inspire others, and effect profound change in the world.

5

Command and Control: Leading with Authority

Leading with authority involves taking on a position of leadership where you have the responsibility to guide and influence individuals or teams within an organization or group. It signifies not only a position of power but also the accountability that comes with it. Here, we delve into the concept of leading with authority and its significance in achieving goals and fostering a positive impact. Command and control is a leadership style and approach that emphasizes centralized authority, hierarchical structure, and a clear chain of command. It is often associated with military organizations, but its principles have applications in various fields, including business and emergency management. Here's more information about command and control leadership:

Key Characteristics:

Centralized Decision-Making: In command and control leadership, decision-making authority is concentrated at the top of the hierarchy. Leaders at the top have the final say on significant matters, and their directives are expected to be followed without deviation.

Hierarchical Structure: Command and control organizations have a well-defined hierarchical structure, with individuals and teams arranged in a clear order. Each level of the hierarchy has specific responsibilities and authority.

Clear Chain of Command: There is a defined chain of command that outlines the flow of communication and decision-making. This chain ensures that information and directives move efficiently up and down the hierarchy.

Discipline and Obedience: Command and control leadership places a strong emphasis on discipline and obedience. Members of the organization are expected to follow orders promptly and without question.

Efficiency and Predictability: The approach seeks to create a highly efficient and predictable environment where processes are standardized and tasks are executed according to established procedures.

Applications:

Military: Command and control is most commonly associated with military organizations, where clear authority, discipline, and efficient communication are critical for ensuring mission success and the safety of personnel.

Emergency Services: Fire departments, police forces, and other emergency services often rely on command and control structures during crisis situations to ensure a coordinated response.

Corporate Leadership: Some business organizations adopt elements of command and control leadership to maintain order and structure, especially in highly regulated industries or during periods of crisis.

Advantages:

Clarity and Accountability: Command and control leadership provides clear lines of authority, which can reduce ambiguity and ensure accountability.

Efficiency: The approach can enhance efficiency by streamlining processes and decision-making.

Crisis Management: In emergency situations, command and control leadership can help maintain order and facilitate rapid responses.

Challenges:

Inflexibility: The rigid nature of command and control leadership may hinder adaptability in rapidly changing environments.

Creativity and Innovation: It may stifle creativity and innovation because it often relies on established procedures.

Employee Engagement: Employees in command and control organizations may feel dis-empowered or disengaged if they have little input into decision-making.

Balancing Command and Control:

Effective leaders often balance the command and control approach with more participate and empowering leadership styles to foster creativity and adaptability while maintaining order and structure.

In summary, command and control leadership is characterized by centralized authority, hierarchical structure, and strict discipline. While it has its advantages in maintaining order and accountability, it may also face challenges related to adaptability and employee engagement. Leaders must balance these characteristics to suit the specific needs of their organization and its environment.

6

Building Alliances and Collaborative Partnerships

The alliances formed on the battlefield can spell the difference between victory and defeat. Similarly, life often calls for the forging of alliances and partnerships. In Chapter 6, we delve into the intricate dynamics of building collaborative relationships. You'll discover how to establish strong, mutually beneficial connections, working in synergy with others to achieve common goals. Building alliances and collaborative partnerships is a strategic approach that involves forming connections and relationships with individuals, organizations, or groups to achieve common goals and create mutually beneficial outcomes. These relationships can be instrumental in various contexts, from business to diplomacy, and are essential in fostering success through cooperation. Here, we explore the significance and key aspects of building alliances and partnerships.

Defining Alliances and Collaborative Partnerships

Alliances and collaborative partnerships involve establishing cooperative relationships with the aim of achieving shared objectives. Key elements of this approach include:

Hared Goals: Partners in alliances and partnerships work toward common objectives or interests, aligning their efforts for mutual benefit.

Mutual Benefit: The cooperation is expected to bring advantages to all parties involved, creating a win-win situation.

Resource Sharing: Partners may share resources, knowledge, expertise, or access to networks, enhancing their collective capabilities.

Trust and Commitment: Trust is a fundamental component of successful alliances. Commitment to the partnership's success is essential.

Significance in Achieving Success

Building alliances and collaborative partnerships are significant for several reasons:

Leveraging Strengths: Partners can leverage each other's strengths and resources, resulting in increased efficiency and effectiveness in achieving their goals.

Risk Mitigation: Collaborative efforts can help distribute and mitigate risks among the partners, making it easier to handle challenges and uncertainties.

Access to New Markets: Partnerships can provide access to new markets, customers, or opportunities that might be challenging to reach individually.

Knowledge and Innovation: Collaborative partnerships can foster knowledge sharing and innovation, leading to the development of new ideas and solutions.

Economic and Resource Efficiency: Sharing resources, costs, and responsibilities can lead to economic and resource efficiency.

Key Aspects of Building Alliances and Collaborative Partnerships

Identification of Common Goals: Partners must have a clear understanding of their shared objectives and ensure alignment before entering into a partnership.

Trust and Relationship Building: Trust is the foundation of successful partnerships. Building strong relationships with partners is essential for ongoing collaboration.

Open Communication: Effective communication is vital for the success of any partnership. Partners must maintain open, honest, and transparent communication.

Shared Values and Vision: Partnerships are more likely to succeed when the involved parties share similar values and a common vision for the future.

Agreement and Commitment: Formal agreements, contracts, or memoranda of understanding help solidify the partnership and outline roles, responsibilities, and expectations.

Challenges and Growth

Building alliances and collaborative partnerships can be challenging. Partners may have different interests, expectations, or methods of operation. Managing these differences, addressing conflicts, and maintaining commitment to the partnership can be demanding. However, these challenges provide opportunities for personal and organizational growth, including the development of negotiation and conflict resolution skills.

In conclusion, building alliances and collaborative partnerships is a strategic approach that facilitates the achievement of common goals and fosters success through cooperation. By leveraging shared resources, knowledge, and expertise, partners can enhance their capabilities and create opportunities for mutual growth and advancement.

7

Inspiring Loyalty and Motivation

Inspiring loyalty and motivation among individuals or within a team is a vital aspect of effective leadership. This involves cultivating a work environment where people feel committed, engaged, and enthusiastic about their roles. Here, we explore the significance and key elements of inspiring loyalty and motivation. Loyalty and motivation are the lifeblood of successful leadership. In this chapter, we investigate the subtle art of inspiring unwavering loyalty in those you lead. Drawing from military wisdom, you'll uncover strategies to motivate and encourage others, fostering a sense of dedication that leads to collective triumph.

Defining Loyalty and Motivation

Loyalty: Loyalty in a professional context refers to the commitment and dedication that individuals have towards an organization, a leader, or a team. Loyal individuals are dedicated to the organization's mission, values, and goals and they often go above and beyond in their efforts to support those objectives.

Motivation: Motivation involves the drive and enthusiasm that individuals bring to their work. It is the internal or external force that encourages people to take action, set and achieve goals, and put forth their best efforts.

Significance in Achieving Success

Inspiring loyalty and motivation is significant for several reasons:

Increased Productivity: Motivated individuals tend to be more productive, resulting in improved performance and the accomplishment of organizational goals.

Retention of Talent: Loyalty often leads to employee retention. When individuals feel committed and valued, they are more likely to stay with the organization, reducing turnover and associated costs.

Enhanced Creativity and Innovation: Motivated and loyal team members are more likely to contribute new ideas and innovative solutions to problems.

Positive Work Environment: A motivated and loyal workforce contributes to a positive work environment, which, in turn, can attract more talent and foster collaboration.

Adaptability and Resilience: Motivated and loyal individuals are more adaptable and resilient, making them better equipped to navigate challenges and changes.

Key Elements of Inspiring Loyalty and Motivation

Leading by Example: Leaders who exhibit dedication, commitment, and enthusiasm can inspire similar qualities in their team members.

Effective Communication: Open, honest, and transparent communication is essential for motivating and inspiring loyalty. Leaders should articulate the organization's goals and values clearly.

Recognition and Rewards: Acknowledging and rewarding exceptional performance or dedication can reinforce loyalty and motivation.

Professional Growth: Providing opportunities for learning and advancement encourages motivation and loyalty as individuals see a future within the organization.

Empowerment and Autonomy: Allowing individuals to have a degree of autonomy and control in their work can foster motivation and loyalty.

Support and Feedback: Providing support, guidance, and constructive feedback is crucial for maintaining motivation and loyalty.

Challenges and Growth:

Inspiring loyalty and motivation may face challenges related to individual differences, competing priorities, and external factors that affect individuals' commitment and enthusiasm. Overcoming these challenges requires continuous effort, adaptability, and a commitment to fostering a positive work environment.

In conclusion, inspiring loyalty and motivation is a cornerstone of effective leadership. By cultivating an environment where individuals feel dedicated, engaged, and enthusiastic about their work, leaders can promote productivity, retention, creativity, and resilience, ultimately contributing to the achievement of organizational success.

43

8

Effective Communication: Winning Hearts and Minds

In the pursuit of success, effective communication is a powerful tool that can influence and inspire. Here are key strategies to achieve success through winning hearts and minds with effective communication:

Authenticity and Genuine Connection:
- Be authentic in your communication. People are more likely to connect with and trust individuals who are genuine.
- Share personal stories and experiences to create a human connection and resonate with your audience.

Active Listening:
- Practice active listening to understand others' perspectives and concerns.
- Show genuine interest, ask clarifying questions, and paraphrase to confirm understanding.

Clarity and Conciseness:
- Communicate with clarity and conciseness. Avoid jargon and unnecessary complexity.

- Clearly articulate your message to ensure it is easily understood by a diverse audience.

Empathy and Understanding:
- Cultivate empathy to understand the emotions and needs of others.
- Acknowledge and validate others' feelings, demonstrating that you care about their well-being.

Adaptability and Flexibility:
- Be adaptable in your communication style to accommodate different personalities and situations.
- Adjust your approach based on the needs and preferences of your audience.

Storytelling:
- Harness the power of storytelling to convey messages in a compelling and memorable way.
- Craft narratives that evoke emotions and illustrate key points to make your communication more impactful.

Credibility and Trustworthiness:
- Build and maintain credibility by delivering on promises and consistently demonstrating integrity.
- People are more likely to follow and support those they trust.

Inclusive Communication include:
Consistency in Messaging:

- Maintain consistency in your communication, ensuring that your messages align with your values and goals.
- Consistency builds a reliable and trustworthy reputation.

Humble Leadership:
- Embrace humility in leadership communication. Admitting mistakes and expressing vulnerability can build trust and authenticity.
- Humble leaders are often more relatable and approachable.

Celebrating Success Together:
- Share successes collectively to foster a sense of unity and teamwork.
- Acknowledge and appreciate the contributions of others, reinforcing a positive and collaborative culture.

Continuous Improvement:
- Seek feedback on your communication and be open to continuous improvement.
- Adapt your communication style based on feedback and evolving circumstances.

By implementing these strategies, you can create a communication style that not only conveys information effectively but also inspires and engages others. Winning hearts and minds through effective communication is not just about conveying a message; it's about creating connections, fostering collaboration, and ultimately achieving success together.

47

III

Resilience and Perseverance

Resilience and perseverance are essential qualities that empower individuals to face challenges, setbacks, and adversity with strength and determination. They are the twin pillars of personal growth and success, providing the ability to bounce back from adversity and continue striving for one's goals. Here, we explore the significance and key aspects of resilience and perseverance.

9

Defining Resilience and Perseverance

Resilience and perseverance are essential qualities that empower individuals to face challenges, setbacks, and adversity with strength and determination. They are the twin pillars of personal growth and success, providing the ability to bounce back from adversity and continue striving for one's goals. Here, we explore the significance and key aspects of resilience and perseverance.

Defining Resilience and Perseverance:

Resilience: Resilience is the ability to withstand, adapt to, or recover from adverse situations. It involves the capacity to remain composed and maintain mental and emotional well-being in the face of adversity.

Perseverance: Perseverance is the quality of persisting in one's efforts despite difficulties, obstacles, or discouragement. It is the determination to keep working towards one's goals, even when facing setbacks.

Life, much like a battlefield, often presents formidable challenges and unexpected adversities.

The principles of resilience and perseverance, honed on the frontlines of history's most daunting conflicts, offer invaluable guidance in navigating these trials. Part III is a compass that guides us in the quest to overcome adversity and emerge stronger on the other side.

Facing adversity is an inevitable part of life, and it often provides valuable lessons that can shape one's character and future success. The experiences of those who have confronted adversity head-on can offer important insights and guidance for navigating challenges. Here, we delve into some key lessons from the frontlines of adversity.

Lesson 1: Resilience is a Powerful Asset

One of the most significant lessons from facing adversity is the power of resilience. Resilience is the ability to bounce back from setbacks and maintain mental and emotional well-being in the face of adversity. Those who have weathered storms have often emerged stronger and more adaptable. Resilience enables individuals to endure difficulties, learn from them, and become better equipped to face future challenges.

Lesson 2: Perspective Matters

Adversity has a way of reframing one's perspective on life. When facing difficult circumstances, individuals often gain a greater appreciation for the things that truly matter, such as family, health, and personal values. Adversity can help individuals prioritize their lives, focusing on what brings genuine happiness and fulfillment.

Lesson 3: Adaptability is Key

Adversity often requires individuals to adapt and embrace change. The ability to adjust to new circumstances and find innovative solutions is a valuable skill acquired through challenging experiences. Adaptable individuals can transform adversity into an opportunity for growth and learning.

Lesson 4: Seek Support and Connection

Facing adversity is not something that needs to be done in isolation. Those who have navigated difficult times often stress the importance of seeking support from friends, family, or a support network. Connecting with others can provide emotional and practical assistance, making the journey through adversity more manageable.

Lesson 5: Perseverance Leads to Progress

Perseverance is the determination to continue working toward one's goals despite obstacles. People who have confronted adversity have often found that persistence is a key factor in making progress. Perseverance helps maintain a focus on long-term objectives and fosters personal growth.

Lesson 6: Vulnerability is Strength

Adversity can strip away the facades and pretenses, allowing individuals to embrace vulnerability. Sharing one's challenges and seeking help when needed is a sign of strength, not weakness. Vulnerability can lead to deeper connections with others and the discovery of shared experiences.

Lesson 7: Learning and Growth Are Inevitable

Adversity is a powerful teacher. Those who have faced adversity often emerge with valuable insights, new skills, and a broader perspective on life. Challenges can lead to personal growth, increased wisdom, and a greater capacity to empathize with the struggles of others.

Lesson 8: Hope and Optimism Can Prevail

Despite the difficulties encountered in the face of adversity, hope and optimism can endure. Those who have navigated adversity often emphasize the importance of maintaining a positive outlook and believing in the possibility of a brighter future.

In conclusion, facing adversity is a profound life experience that can impart invaluable lessons. Resilience, adaptability, perseverance, and the ability to connect with others are just a few of the qualities that individuals can develop when confronting challenges. Adversity often becomes a catalyst for personal growth, shaping character and providing the wisdom to navigate life's complexities.

10

Facing Adversity: Lessons from the Frontlines

In this chapter, we delve into the profound insights drawn from the crucible of battle and learn how to face adversity with courage and determination. As warriors adapt to ever-changing conditions on the battlefield, we too can harness the strength to confront life's most formidable challenges, understanding that adversity is a potent catalyst for personal growth.

When individuals confront adversity, they often gain invaluable insights and lessons that shape their character and provide guidance for navigating challenges. The experiences of those who have weathered life's storms offer profound wisdom for overcoming adversity and emerging stronger. Here are some key lessons from the frontlines of adversity:

Lesson 1:Resilience is a Superpower

Adversity underscores the incredible power of resilience. Resilience is the ability to bounce back from setbacks, maintain emotional strength, and adapt to challenging circumstances. Those who have faced adversity understand that setbacks are not the end but an opportunity for personal growth and transformation. Resilience enables individuals to endure, learn, and emerge even more robust.

Lesson 2:Perspective Shapes Reality

Adversity has a way of reshaping one's perspective on life. When facing difficult circumstances, individuals often reevaluate their priorities and discover what truly matters. Adversity teaches us that material possessions and superficial concerns pale in comparison to family, health, relationships, and personal values. It reminds us to focus on what brings genuine happiness and fulfillment.

Lesson 3:Adaptability is the Key to Survival

Adversity requires adaptability. Those who confront adversity learn that change is inevitable, and the ability to adapt is crucial. Adaptable individuals can pivot, embrace new strategies, and find innovative solutions to challenges. They view adversity as an opportunity for personal and professional growth.

Lesson 4:Seek Support and Forge Connections

Adversity need not be faced alone. The importance of seeking support from friends, family, or a support network cannot be overstated. Connecting with others provides emotional solace and practical assistance, making the journey through adversity more manageable. The bonds formed during tough times often become the bedrock of enduring relationships.

Lesson 5:Perseverance Leads to Progress

Perseverance is the fuel that keeps us moving forward despite obstacles. Individuals who have navigated adversity understand that persistence is essential for progress. Perseverance is what allows them to maintain a steadfast focus on long-term objectives and grow stronger with each step.

Lesson 6:Vulnerability is a Strength

Adversity often strips away pretenses and facades, revealing the strength in vulnerability. Sharing one's challenges and seeking help are acts of courage, not weakness. Vulnerability fosters genuine connections with others and highlights the universality of human struggles. It is through vulnerability that people find understanding and support.

Lesson 7:Learning and Growth Are Inevitable

Adversity is a profound teacher. Those who have faced adversity emerge with newfound wisdom, skills, and a broader perspective on life. Challenges lead to personal growth, a deeper understanding of oneself, and an increased capacity to empathize with others' struggles.

Lesson 8:Hope and Optimism Endure

Despite the darkness of adversity, hope and optimism can persist. Those who have endured challenges stress the importance of maintaining a positive outlook and believing in the possibility of a brighter future. They understand that while adversity is difficult, it is not insurmountable, and better days can lie ahead.

In conclusion, facing adversity is a profound life experience that imparts invaluable lessons. Resilience, adaptability, perseverance, and the ability to connect with others are just a few of the qualities that individuals can develop when confronting adversity. These lessons serve as a compass, guiding individuals through the storms of life and leading them toward greater strength and wisdom.

11

Mental Toughness and Emotional Resilience

Mental toughness, a hallmark of seasoned warriors, forms the crux of Chapter 10. We explore the strategies to fortify one's psychological resilience, equipping ourselves to endure life's storms with grace. By nurturing emotional resilience, we can withstand stress and upheaval, emerging unscathed and strengthened by adversity.

Mental toughness and emotional resilience are qualities that empower individuals to withstand and overcome adversity, stress, and challenges. They serve as the foundation for a strong and resilient mindset, enabling individuals to navigate life's ups and downs with courage and fortitude. Here, we explore the significance and key aspects of mental toughness and emotional resilience.

Defining Mental Toughness and Emotional Resilience:

Mental Toughness: Mental toughness refers to the ability to remain focused, determined, and resilient in the face of adversity. It involves maintaining a strong and positive mindset, even when confronted with challenging situations.

Emotional Resilience: Emotional resilience is the capacity to bounce back from emotional setbacks, stress, and difficult experiences. It includes the ability to manage and regulate emotions effectively.

Significance in Achieving Success:

Mental toughness and emotional resilience are vital for various reasons:

Overcoming Adversity: Life presents a myriad of challenges, setbacks, and unexpected obstacles. Mental toughness and emotional resilience help individuals endure, adapt, and emerge stronger from these experiences.

Personal Growth: Confronting adversity is a catalyst for personal growth and self-discovery. Mental toughness and emotional resilience enable individuals to learn from difficulties and become more resilient.

Optimal Performance: These qualities enhance an individual's performance and productivity. They enable individuals to stay focused, make effective decisions, and maintain a positive outlook, even under pressure.

Healthy Relationships: Mental toughness and emotional resilience contribute to healthier and more fulfilling relationships. They enable individuals to communicate effectively, manage conflicts, and provide emotional support.

Enhanced Well-being: Emotional resilience leads to emotional well-being by helping individuals manage stress, anxiety, and other emotional challenges effectively.

Key Elements of Mental Toughness:

Positive Mindset: Mental toughness is closely associated with maintaining a positive and resilient mindset, which enables individuals to face adversity with determination.

Focus and Determination: Individuals with mental toughness maintain unwavering focus on their goals and exhibit a strong sense of determination.

Adaptability: Mental toughness is linked to adaptability, allowing individuals to adjust to changing circumstances and overcome challenges effectively.

Problem-Solving Skills: Mental toughness involves the ability to analyze problems, identify solutions, and take action to address challenges.

Optimism: Maintaining a sense of optimism is vital for mental toughness, as it helps individuals face adversity with hope and a can-do attitude.

Key Elements of Emotional Resilience:

Emotional Regulation: Emotional resilience involves the ability to manage and regulate emotions effectively, preventing them from overwhelming or controlling an individual.

Self-Awareness: Understanding one's own emotions and recognizing emotional triggers is an essential component of emotional resilience.

Coping Strategies: Emotional resilience includes the development of healthy coping strategies to manage stress and emotional challenges.

Social Support: Building a network of supportive relationships is crucial for emotional resilience, as it provides a source of emotional solace and encouragement.

Self-Compassion: Being kind and compassionate to oneself in times of difficulty is an integral aspect of emotional resilience.

Developing mental toughness and emotional resilience can be challenged by adverse circumstances, self-doubt, and external pressures. However, these challenges provide opportunities for personal growth, self-improvement, and the development of mental and emotional strength.

69

12

The Art of Endurance: Never Giving Up

Endurance, a trait revered by warriors through the ages, takes center stage in this chapter. You'll uncover the power of tenacity, the unyielding spirit that fuels us to keep moving forward, even when the odds seem insurmountable. Through the lessons of the battlefield, we gain the wisdom to persevere in the face of seemingly insurmountable obstacles. It is also the art of persevering through challenges, setbacks, and obstacles, even when the odds seem insurmountable. It's a quality that goes hand-in-hand with mental toughness and emotional resilience, representing an unwavering commitment to never giving up. Here, we delve into the significance and key aspects of the art of endurance.

Significance of Endurance:

Endurance holds great significance for a variety of reasons:

Overcoming Adversity: Life is riddled with adversities and trials. Endurance empowers individuals to face these difficulties head-on, never losing sight of their goals.

Resilience: Endurance contributes to resilience. It's the ability to keep going when everything seems to be working against you, ultimately leading to personal growth and inner strength.

Achieving Long-Term Goals: Many worthwhile endeavors require sustained effort over time. Endurance ensures individuals stay on course, even when faced with obstacles, and reach their long-term objectives.

Optimal Performance: In various aspects of life, whether in personal relationships or professional endeavors, endurance leads to optimal performance.

It helps individuals remain focused and maintain a positive outlook, even in challenging situations.

Inspiration to Others: Those who endure through hardships often serve as a source of inspiration to others. Their determination and commitment can motivate and uplift those around them.

Key Aspects of Endurance:

Unwavering Commitment: The art of endurance is rooted in unwavering commitment to one's goals. It means staying dedicated, regardless of the challenges that arise.

Persistence: Persistence is a core element of endurance. It's the refusal to quit, even when progress is slow, and difficulties are abundant.

Optimism: Maintaining an optimistic outlook is crucial for enduring through adversity. Believing in the possibility of a positive outcome keeps one motivated.

Adaptability: Adaptability is a key aspect of endurance, as it allows individuals to adjust their strategies and approaches when necessary.

Coping Strategies: Developing healthy coping strategies to manage stress and emotional challenges is essential for enduring through difficult times.

Focus on Long-Term Objectives: The art of endurance involves a focus on long-term objectives, even when short-term setbacks occur.

Endurance can be tested by numerous challenges, including self-doubt, external pressures, and unexpected circumstances. These challenges provide opportunities for personal growth, resilience, and the development of mental and emotional strength. Overcoming adversity often results in a deeper sense of self-awareness and an increased ability to empathize with the struggles of others.

In conclusion, the art of endurance is a testament to the human spirit's ability to persist through adversity and overcome life's challenges. By maintaining unwavering commitment, persistence, and a positive outlook, individuals can endure and ultimately achieve their goals, serving as an inspiration to those around them. Endurance is not just a quality; it's an art that embodies the essence of never giving up.

13

Managing Stress and Burnout

Stress and burnout are foes faced not only by soldiers in the heat of battle but by individuals in the modern world. This examines how to effectively manage stress and prevent burnout, drawing from the techniques used to maintain a soldier's psychological well-being in the most trying of circumstances. Managing stress and preventing burnout is crucial for maintaining mental and physical well-being in today's fast-paced world. The demands of modern life can be overwhelming, but effective stress management strategies can help individuals stay balanced, healthy, and focused. Here, we explore the significance and key aspects of managing stress and preventing burnout.

In Part III, we delve deep into the tenets of resilience and perseverance, gleaned from the crucible of war. Just as military commanders and soldiers endure the harshest conditions, emerge from adversity unbroken, and sustain their resolve in the face of relentless challenges, these chapters offer practical wisdom for weathering the storms of life. By embracing these principles, you arm yourself with the fortitude to not only survive but to thrive, emerging victorious in the most trying circumstances.

Significance of Managing Stress and Burnout:

Managing stress and preventing burnout is significant for several reasons:

Mental and Physical Health: Chronic stress and burnout can lead to a range of health problems, including anxiety, depression, cardiovascular issues, and compromised immune function.

Optimal Performance: Effective stress management enhances cognitive function, decision-making, and productivity, allowing individuals to perform at their best in various areas of life.

Positive Relationships: High-stress levels can strain personal and professional relationships. Managing stress promotes healthier interactions and communication.

Resilience: Effective stress management contributes to resilience, helping individuals bounce back from adversity and cope with challenges effectively.

Life Satisfaction: Reducing stress and preventing burnout can lead to a greater sense of life satisfaction and happiness.

Key Aspects of Managing Stress:

Identify Stressors: The first step in managing stress is to identify the sources of stress in your life. This awareness helps you take targeted action to reduce stress.

Time Management: Effective time management allows individuals to prioritize tasks and activities, reducing the feeling of being overwhelmed.

Physical Activity: Regular physical exercise is an excellent stress reliever, releasing endorphins that boost mood and reduce stress.

Relaxation Techniques: Incorporating relaxation techniques such as deep breathing, meditation, and mindfulness can help individuals manage stress and achieve a sense of calm.

Social Support: Maintaining a support network of friends and family provides emotional solace and practical assistance during stressful times.

Key Aspects of Preventing Burnout:

Set Boundaries: Establish clear boundaries between work and personal life to prevent overexertion and burnout.

Take Breaks: Regular breaks during the workday and time for relaxation are crucial for preventing burnout.

Self-Care: Prioritize self-care activities that promote relaxation and well-being, such as hobbies, exercise, and sufficient sleep.

Delegate Tasks: Don't hesitate to delegate tasks or ask for help when needed. Sharing responsibilities can reduce the risk of burnout.

Regular Check-Ins: Continuously monitor your stress levels and take action if you notice signs of burnout, such as fatigue, irritability, or a loss of interest in activities.

Challenges and Growth:

Managing stress and preventing burnout can be challenging, as it often involves changing long-standing habits and seeking support when needed.

Challenges may include time constraints, competing priorities, and external pressures. However, overcoming these challenges provides opportunities for personal growth, self-improvement, and the development of resilience.

In conclusion, managing stress and preventing burnout is essential for maintaining a healthy and balanced life. By identifying stressors, implementing stress management strategies, and practicing self-care, individuals can build resilience, improve well-being, and perform at their best, even in the face of life's demands. when facing overwhelming stress or burnout.

IV

Time Management and Productivity

In the dynamic tapestry of existence, the judicious allocation of time and the art of productivity stand as linchpins to success. Drawing inspiration from the disciplined strategies of military life, Part IV offers a compass to navigate the demanding world of commitments and aspirations. When individuals learn to use their time efficiently, they can accomplish more, reduce stress, and maintain a healthy work-life balance.

14

Significance of Time Management and Productivity

The significance of time management and productivity cannot be overstated in today's fast-paced world. These skills are essential for personal and professional success, and their importance can be summarized in several key points:

Optimal Resource Utilization: Efficient time management ensures that individuals make the best use of their time and resources, whether at work, in education, or in daily life.

Stress Reduction: Properly managing time and being productive can reduce stress by preventing the feeling of being overwhelmed by tasks and deadlines.

Achieving Goals: Time management helps individuals set and achieve their goals, whether they are related to career advancement, personal development, or creative pursuits.

Work-Life Balance: Good time management allows individuals to allocate time for both work and personal life, promoting a healthier balance and well-being.

Professional Success: Productivity and time management skills are highly valued in the professional world, as they contribute to efficiency and effectiveness in the workplace.

Key Aspects of Time Management:

Setting Goals: Begin by setting clear, achievable goals. Knowing what you want to accomplish helps you prioritize your tasks.

Prioritization: Determine the most important tasks and allocate your time and effort accordingly. The Eisenhower Matrix, which categorizes tasks as urgent/important, can be a helpful tool.

Planning: Develop a daily or weekly plan to outline tasks, deadlines, and milestones. Planning helps you stay organized and on track.

Time Blocking: Allocate specific time blocks for different tasks or activities. Time blocking ensures that you have dedicated periods for focused work.

Eliminating Distractions: Identify common distractions and work to minimize them. This may involve turning off notifications, creating a clutter-free workspace, or using website blockers.

Key Aspects of Productivity:

Focus and Concentration: Train your ability to focus on tasks without getting sidetracked. Techniques like the Pomodoro Technique can help enhance concentration.

Effective Task Management: Use task management tools and techniques to track your tasks, set deadlines, and monitor progress.

Delegation: Delegate tasks to others when possible, freeing up your time to focus on higher-priority responsibilities.

Continuous Learning: Invest in personal and professional development to enhance your skills and knowledge, which can lead to increased productivity.

Self-Care: Take breaks, maintain a healthy work-life balance, and ensure you get adequate sleep and exercise. A well-rested and healthy individual is more productive.

Challenges and Growth:

Challenges in time management and productivity often include procrastination, lack of motivation, and the temptation of distractions. Overcoming these challenges requires discipline, self-awareness, and the willingness to seek assistance or guidance when needed.

In conclusion, time management and productivity are essential skills for achieving personal and professional success. By setting goals, prioritizing tasks, and adopting effective time management and productivity strategies, individuals can maximize their efficiency, reduce stress, and work toward their desired outcomes.

15

The Urgency of Time: Seizing Opportunities

Time is a finite resource, a fleeting and irretrievable asset much like the critical moments on a battlefield. Chapter 14 underscores the significance of time management, emphasizing the importance of seizing opportunities when they arise. Discover the strategies to maximize your use of time, ensuring that you make the most of each day, each hour, and each precious moment.

The urgency of time brings seizing opportunities i.e the most precious and irreplaceable resource, can either propel us toward our goals or slip through our fingers unnoticed. In this chapter, we delve into the urgency of time and the critical importance of seizing opportunities when they arise. Key concepts explored include:

Mindful Time Management: Discover the principles of mindful time management, a practice that empowers you to allocate your time to the most meaningful and impactful activities.

Proactive Decision-Making: Learn how to make decisions efficiently, embracing opportunities as they present themselves rather than procrastinating or hesitating.

The Power of Timing: Understand how the timing of your actions can significantly impact your chances of success. Delve into strategies for recognizing the right moment to act.

Eliminating Time Wasters: Identify and eliminate common time-wasting activities and distractions that hinder productivity and steal precious moments from your day.

Key Aspects of Seizing Opportunities:

Awareness: Being aware of opportunities is the first step. This involves staying informed, being curious, and recognizing potential openings.

Courage: Seizing opportunities often requires courage. It means stepping out of one's comfort zone, taking risks, and facing the fear of the unknown.

Pro-activity: Being proactive is essential. It involves taking the initiative and not waiting for opportunities to come to you.

Readiness: To seize opportunities, individuals should be prepared. This means developing the skills and knowledge necessary to make the most of an opportunity when it arises.

Time Management: Effective time management ensures that individuals have the time and flexibility to seize opportunities as they present themselves.

Networking: Building a network of contacts can lead to various opportunities, both personally and professionally.

In conclusion, the urgency of time serves as a reminder of the finite nature of life and the importance of making the most of every moment. Seizing opportunities is the key to personal and professional growth, fulfilling relationships, and career advancement. By being aware, courageous, proactive, and prepared, individuals can make the most of the opportunities that come their way and lead a more fulfilling life.

16

Prioritization and Resource Allocation

Just as military commanders allocate resources judiciously to achieve their objectives; this chapter imparts the wisdom of prioritization and resource management. You'll explore the principles of setting priorities and allocating resources effectively, whether in your professional or personal life. By doing so, you empower yourself to focus on what truly matters and make the best use of your available resources.

Prioritization and resource allocation are fundamental aspects of effective decision-making, both in personal and professional contexts. These skills are vital for ensuring that limited resources, such as time, money, and energy, are used efficiently and effectively. Here, we explore the significance of prioritization and resource allocation and their key aspects.

Significance of Prioritization and Resource Allocation:

Efficiency: Prioritization and resource allocation are essential for ensuring that resources are used efficiently. By focusing on high-priority tasks or projects, individuals and organizations can maximize their productivity and effectiveness.

Goal Achievement: Effective prioritization and resource allocation contribute to goal achievement. When resources are allocated to the most important and strategic activities, it's more likely that objectives will be met.

Time Management: Prioritization plays a crucial role in time management. By identifying the most important tasks, individuals can make the best use of their time and reduce the risk of wasting it on less critical activities.

Stress Reduction: Effective prioritization and resource allocation help reduce stress by preventing individuals from feeling overwhelmed by a multitude of tasks or commitments.

Strategic Decision-Making: In the business world, prioritization and resource allocation are central to strategic decision-making. They guide organizations in selecting projects, investments, and initiatives that align with their long-term goals.

Key Aspects of Prioritization:

Goal Setting: Prioritization begins with setting clear goals. Individuals or organizations must have a clear understanding of what they want to achieve.

Task Assessment: Each task or project should be assessed in terms of its importance and urgency. Tools like the Eisenhower Matrix can be helpful for this purpose.

Ranking: Once tasks are assessed, they can be ranked in order of priority. This ranking guides decision-making by highlighting which activities should be tackled first.

Reassessment: Priorities may change over time, so regular reassessment is important. As circumstances evolve, individuals should adjust their priorities accordingly.

Delegation: For tasks that are not top priorities or that can be handled by others, delegation is a valuable skill. Delegating tasks frees up time and resources for more critical activities.

Key Aspects of Resource Allocation:

Resource Evaluation: Organizations and individuals need to evaluate the resources available, including time, money, personnel, and technology.

Alignment with Priorities: Resources should be allocated to activities that align with the established priorities and goals.

Budgeting: Financial resources should be budgeted effectively to ensure that they cover the expenses associated with high-priority projects or initiatives.

Monitoring and Adjustment: Ongoing monitoring of resource allocation is important to ensure that resources are used optimally. Adjustments may be necessary as circumstances change.

Risk Management: Consideration of potential risks and contingencies is vital in resource allocation to mitigate unexpected challenges.

The challenges in prioritization and resource allocation often involve making tough decisions, managing limited resources, and handling unexpected changes. Overcoming these challenges provides opportunities for personal and professional growth, as individuals and organizations develop adaptability, resilience, and improved decision-making skills.

In conclusion, prioritization and resource allocation are essential skills that guide effective decision-making and resource management. By setting clear priorities,

99

17

Efficiency and Productivity: Doing More with Less

Efficiency is a hallmark of military strategy, where achieving more with fewer resources can be a decisive advantage. Chapter 15 reveals the strategies for optimizing your efficiency and productivity. Learn how to streamline your processes, eliminate time-wasting activities, and accomplish more with the same or fewer resources. Efficiency and productivity are also paramount in today's fast-paced world, where individuals and organizations strive to accomplish more with limited resources. These skills are crucial for optimizing performance, achieving goals, and maintaining a competitive edge. Here, we explore the significance of efficiency and productivity and their key aspects.

Significance of Efficiency and Productivity:

Resource Optimization: Efficiency and productivity involve making the most of available resources, whether they are time, money, or energy. This optimization is essential for success in personal and professional life.

Goal Attainment: Efficient and productive individuals are more likely to achieve their goals and objectives. They can tackle more tasks and projects, moving closer to their desired outcomes.

Competitive Advantage: In the business world, organizations that prioritize efficiency and productivity can gain a competitive advantage. They can offer products or services at lower costs and with higher quality.

Time Management: Efficiency and productivity are fundamental to time management. They help individuals make the best use of their time, reducing stress and preventing the feeling of being overwhelmed.

Innovation: Efficient and productive individuals and organizations often seek innovative solutions to improve their processes and find new ways to do more with less.

Key Aspects of Efficiency:

Streamlining Processes: Identifying and eliminating unnecessary steps in processes can significantly improve efficiency.

Time Management: Effective time management is essential for efficiency. This includes setting priorities, avoiding distractions, and making the best use of available time.

Automation: Automating repetitive tasks and processes can save time and increase efficiency.

Resource Allocation: Allocating resources, such as personnel, budget, and technology, optimally contributes to efficiency.

Continuous Improvement: Striving for continuous improvement is a key aspect of efficiency. Regularly evaluating processes and seeking ways to enhance them is vital.

Key Aspects of Productivity:

Task Management: Effective task management ensures that tasks are completed systematically and in a timely manner.

Goal Setting: Setting clear and achievable goals is crucial for productivity. It provides direction and motivation.

Focus and Concentration: The ability to focus on tasks without being distracted is a significant aspect of productivity.

Time Blocking: Allocating specific time blocks for different tasks can boost productivity by creating focused work periods.

Delegation: Delegating tasks to others when possible allows individuals to focus on high-priority activities.

In conclusion, efficiency and productivity are indispensable skills for achieving personal and professional success. By optimizing resource utilization, setting clear goals, and managing time and tasks effectively, individuals and organizations can accomplish more with less, reducing stress and moving closer to their objectives.

105

18

The Value of Rest and Recovery

In the relentless pace of modern life, rest and recovery are often overlooked, yet they are crucial for sustained productivity. In this chapter, you'll delve into the importance of balancing work with periods of rest. Drawing from military insights, you'll learn how to recharge and maintain your physical and mental well-being, ultimately enhancing your overall productivity.

Part IV delves into the intricacies of time management and productivity, drawing inspiration from the disciplined approaches used in military strategy. By embracing these principles, you equip yourself to make the most of your time, prioritize effectively, maximize efficiency, and recognize the vital role of rest and recovery in maintaining a consistently high level of productivity. These teachings provide you with the tools necessary to succeed in both your personal and professional endeavors, fostering a sense of balance, accomplishment, and well-being. Rest and recovery are indispensable for maintaining physical and mental well-being in our fast-paced and often demanding world. The importance of allowing the body and mind to rest cannot be overstated, as it contributes to better health, performance, and overall quality of life. Here, we explore the significance of rest and recovery and their key aspects.

Significance of Rest and Recovery:

Physical Health: Rest and recovery are essential for physical health. They allow the body to repair and regenerate cells, tissues, and muscles, promoting overall wellness.

Mental Health: Mental well-being is closely tied to adequate rest and recovery. It helps reduce stress, anxiety, and symptoms of mental health conditions.

Performance Enhancement: Rest and recovery are crucial for improving performance in various areas of life, including sports, work, and creativity. A well-rested individual is more alert, focused, and productive.

Emotional Balance: Rest and recovery provide a reprieve from the demands of daily life, allowing individuals to recharge emotionally and maintain a balanced state of mind.

Injury Prevention: Adequate rest and recovery help prevent injuries, particularly in athletes and those engaged in physical activities. It allows the body to heal and reduces the risk of overuse injuries.

Key Aspects of Rest and Recovery:

Sleep: Quality sleep is the foundation of rest and recovery. It allows the body to repair, consolidate memories, and rejuvenate.

Relaxation: Engaging in relaxation techniques, such as meditation, deep breathing, and mindfulness, can help individuals unwind and reduce stress.

Downtime: Setting aside regular downtime for leisure activities, hobbies, and spending time with loved ones is essential for overall well-being.

Physical Recovery: For athletes and individuals engaged in physical activities, physical recovery includes strategies like stretching, massage, and proper nutrition.

Mental Breaks: Mental breaks during work or study periods can refresh the mind and enhance focus and productivity.

In our busy lives, it can be challenging to prioritize rest and recovery. The challenges may include time constraints, work-related demands, and societal pressures. However, overcoming these challenges provides opportunities for personal growth and resilience. Learning to establish healthy boundaries and prioritize rest can lead to improved health and a better work-life balance.

In conclusion, the value of rest and recovery cannot be understated. Prioritizing time for sleep, relaxation, and mental breaks is essential for physical and mental health, as well as for enhancing performance and overall quality of life. Rest and recovery are investments in well-being that provide numerous benefits, ultimately leading to a happier and more balanced life.

V

Conflict Resolution and Negotiation

In the complex tapestry of human interaction, conflicts inevitably arise. Drawing insights from the principles of warfare and diplomacy, Part V delves into the art of conflict resolution and negotiation, offering a comprehensive guide for navigating disputes and achieving mutually beneficial agreements. Conflict resolution and negotiation are essential skills that enable individuals to address differences, reach agreements, and build cooperation.

19

Resolution and Negotiation

Conflict resolution and negotiation are two essential processes for achieving cooperation and resolving differences. Let's delve into these processes based on the title "Conflict Resolution and Negotiation: Building Harmony and Cooperation."

Conflict Resolution: Building Harmony

Conflict resolution is the process of addressing disputes, disagreements, or conflicts in a constructive manner to create a harmonious environment. It involves several key aspects:

Active Listening: In the resolution process, active listening is paramount. It entails genuinely hearing and understanding the perspectives, concerns, and emotions of all parties involved.

Empathy: Empathy plays a crucial role in building harmony during conflict resolution. It involves recognizing and validating the feelings and viewpoints of others, which fosters understanding and emotional connection.

Effective Communication: Effective communication is the bridge that enables parties to express their needs, concerns, and expectations clearly and assertively. It is the foundation for constructive dialogue.

Problem Identification: Identifying the underlying causes of conflicts is vital. By pinpointing these root issues, individuals can address the core problems and work toward solutions.

Conflict Resolution Styles: Different situations may call for various conflict resolution styles. Collaborative approaches involve seeking win-win solutions, compromise involves finding middle ground, avoidance may be appropriate when are minor, and accommodation conflicts or competition styles may be necessary depending on the context.

Negotiation: Achieving Cooperation

Negotiation is a dynamic process for achieving cooperation and reaching agreements. It's a central aspect of building harmony and cooperation:

Preparation: Effective negotiation begins with thorough preparation. Parties involved define their goals, understand each other's needs and interests, and anticipate potential areas of compromise.

Effective Communication: Clear, respectful, and persuasive communication is the lifeblood of negotiation. Both parties must be able to express their views, needs, and expectations openly.

Flexibility: Successful negotiation requires a willingness to adapt and find common ground. Flexibility allows for creative problem-solving and the exploration of mutually beneficial solutions.

Conflict Management Skills: Conflict resolution skills often come into play during negotiation. Conflicts may arise during the process, and managing them constructively is key to achieving cooperation.

Incorporating these key aspects of conflict resolution and negotiation into one's approach can facilitate the process of building harmony and cooperation. It involves actively listening, empathizing, effectively communicating, problem-solving, and demonstrating flexibility and patience when working through disputes or when striving to reach mutually beneficial agreements.

By honing these skills, individuals and organizations can foster a more harmonious environment, resolve differences effectively, and achieve cooperation that benefits all parties involved.

Here, we explore the significance of conflict resolution and negotiation and their key aspects.

Significance of Conflict Resolution and Negotiation:

Conflict Management: Conflict is a natural part of human interaction. Conflict resolution helps manage disputes and disagreements constructively, preventing them from escalating into larger issues.

Positive Relationships: Conflict resolution and negotiation are critical for maintaining healthy relationships. Effective conflict management fosters understanding, empathy, and trust among individuals.

Workplace Harmony: In the professional realm, these skills are vital for creating a harmonious work environment. They lead to better teamwork, improved morale, and increased job satisfaction.

Problem Solving: Conflict resolution and negotiation are problem-solving tools. They help individuals identify issues, generate solutions, and make informed decisions.

Achieving Agreements: Negotiation is the process of reaching agreements that benefit all parties involved. It is a key skill in achieving mutual goals.

Key Aspects of Conflict Resolution:

Active Listening: Active listening is essential for understanding the perspectives and concerns of all parties involved in a conflict.

Empathy: Showing empathy allows individuals to relate to others' feelings and perspectives, which can lead to more constructive discussions.

Communication Skills: Effective communication is key to conflict resolution. It involves clear and assertive communication of one's own needs and concerns.

Problem Identification: Identifying the root causes of conflicts is crucial for addressing them effectively.

Conflict Resolution Styles: Individuals may employ various conflict resolution styles, such as collaboration, compromise, avoidance, or accommodation, depending on the situation.

Key Aspects of Negotiation:

Preparation: Effective negotiation starts with thorough preparation, which includes defining goals, understanding the needs of both parties, and considering potential compromises.

Effective Communication: Negotiation relies on clear, respectful, and persuasive communication. Both parties must be able to express their views and needs.

Flexibility: Negotiators should be open to compromise and finding mutually beneficial solutions.

Conflict Management Skills: Conflict resolution skills are often integral to negotiation, as disagreements may arise during the process.

Patience: Negotiation can be a lengthy process. Patience is necessary to work through differences and reach agreements. Conflict resolution and negotiation can be challenging due to emotions, power imbalances, and varying interests. However, overcoming these challenges fosters personal and professional growth, enhancing communication skills, empathy, and problem-solving abilities.

In conclusion, conflict resolution and negotiation are indispensable skills for maintaining positive relationships, resolving disputes, and achieving mutual goals. By actively listening, empathizing, and using effective communication, individuals can create a more harmonious and cooperative environment, both in personal and professional life.

20

Diplomacy and Negotiation: Avoiding Needless

In this chapter, we explore the role of diplomacy and negotiation in avoiding unnecessary conflicts. Understanding that battles, whether on the battlefield or in daily life, can often be prevented through effective communication and negotiation, you'll delve into the following key factors:

Conflict Prevention: Discover strategies to prevent conflicts before they escalate, by addressing issues proactively and seeking peaceful resolutions.

•

The Diplomat's Mindset: Embrace the mindset of a skilled diplomat, who navigates complex situations with tact, grace, and the aim of preserving relationships

•

Negotiation Strategies: Learn the art of negotiation, understanding how to strike deals that benefit all parties' involved and lead to mutually satisfying outcomes.

The title "***Diplomacy and Negotiation: Avoiding Needless Battles***" underscores the importance of using diplomatic strategies and negotiation skills to prevent unnecessary conflicts. In a world where disputes are commonplace, these processes serve as crucial tools for maintaining peace and harmony. Let's explore the significance of diplomacy and negotiation in avoiding needless battles.

Significance of Diplomacy and Negotiation:

Conflict Prevention: Diplomacy and negotiation are proactive approaches that can prevent conflicts from escalating into unnecessary battles. They prioritize peaceful resolution and compromise over confrontation.

Resource Conservation: Needless battles often result in the wastage of valuable resources, including human lives, time, money, and infrastructure. Diplomacy and negotiation preserve these resources.

International Relations: In the realm of international relations, diplomacy plays a pivotal role in preventing conflicts between nations. Negotiations between countries can avoid war and promote cooperation.

Relationship Maintenance: Diplomacy and negotiation are essential for maintaining healthy relationships, both on a personal and international level. These processes facilitate communication, understanding, and empathy, reducing the risk of conflicts.

Problem Solving: Diplomacy and negotiation are effective problem-solving methods. They allow parties to address issues and disputes in a rational and mutually beneficial way.

Key Aspects of Diplomacy:

Communication: Effective diplomatic efforts begin with open and respectful communication. Diplomats must express their viewpoints clearly and listen attentively to the concerns of others.

Negotiation: Diplomacy often involves negotiation. Diplomats seek to find common ground and reach agreements that satisfy the interests of all parties involved.

Conflict Resolution: Diplomacy includes conflict resolution techniques to address disagreements peacefully and constructively.

Mediation: Diplomats may serve as neutral mediators, assisting parties in finding solutions and compromises.

International Diplomacy: On an international level, diplomacy between nations aims to establish and maintain peaceful relationships, prevent conflicts, and promote collaboration.

Key Aspects of Negotiation:

Preparation: Effective negotiation starts with thorough preparation, which includes understanding the interests, priorities, and needs of all parties involved.

Effective Communication: Clear and persuasive communication is essential for successful negotiation. Parties must express their positions, needs, and expectations clearly and respectfully.

Problem Solving: Negotiation is fundamentally a problem-solving process. Parties work together to find creative solutions that address their respective interests and concerns.

Conflict Resolution: Negotiation often includes conflict resolution skills. It allows parties to manage and resolve disputes during the negotiation process.

Compromise: Negotiation requires a willingness to compromise and find mutually acceptable solutions.

By embracing these key aspects of diplomacy and negotiation, individuals and nations can proactively address disputes and disagreements. They prioritize peaceful resolutions, conserve valuable resources, and maintain healthy relationships, ultimately avoiding needless battles. In doing so, they promote peace, cooperation, and mutual understanding on both personal and international fronts.

21

Understanding the Enemy: Psychology in Conflict

Conflict often stems from differences in perception and understanding. This chapter is an exploration of the psychology of conflict, providing valuable insights into understanding the perspectives of others. Key themes include:

Empathy and Perspective-Taking: Discover the power of empathy and perspective-taking in understanding the motivations and feelings of those in conflict.

•

DE-escalation Techniques: Explore techniques to de-escalate conflicts, reduce tension, and create an environment conducive to productive resolution.

Chapter 21 emphasizes the significance of comprehending the psychological aspects of individuals or groups involved in conflicts. This understanding is critical for effective conflict resolution, peace negotiations, and preventing escalation. Let's explore the importance and key aspects of psychology in conflict.

Significance of Understanding Psychology in Conflict:

Conflict Resolution: Understanding the psychological factors at play in a conflict can provide insights into the motivations, fears, and grievances of all parties involved. This knowledge is essential for finding common ground and facilitating resolution.

DE-escalation: By grasping the psychological triggers that contribute to conflict escalation, individuals and organizations can take measures to DE-escalation tensions and prevent further confrontations.

Negotiation: Negotiation processes benefit from an understanding of the psychological drivers that influence decision-making. Knowing what motivates each party can lead to more successful negotiations.

Conflict Prevention: Psychology can be used to identify potential conflicts before they escalate. Recognizing the warning signs and addressing them early can help prevent hostilities.

Humanitarian Efforts: In situations of armed conflict, understanding the psychological impact on civilians, including trauma and stress, is crucial for organizing humanitarian efforts and providing support.

Key Aspects of Psychology in Conflict:

Motivations: Identifying the motivations of individuals or groups in conflict can help predict their actions and tailor approaches to address their needs or desires.

Emotions: Emotions play a central role in conflict. Understanding the emotional states of involved parties can aid in communication, empathy, and DE-escalation.

Perceptions: Different parties in a conflict may perceive the same situation differently. Recognizing these variations can inform strategies for building common ground.

Communication Styles: Different communication styles may hinder or facilitate dialogue in a conflict. Recognizing and adapting to these styles can improve the effectiveness of communication.

Trauma and Healing: Conflict often inflicts emotional and psychological trauma. Recognizing these effects and offering support for healing is essential in post-conflict scenarios.

Cultural Sensitivity: Cultural factors greatly influence psychology in conflict. Being culturally sensitive and aware of cultural nuances can aid in understanding and resolving conflicts.

Understanding the psychological aspects of conflict allows for more informed and empathetic responses, leading to more effective conflict resolution, negotiation, and peace-building efforts. It enables individuals and organizations to address the root causes of conflicts and work towards lasting solutions that take into account the complex interplay of human emotions and motivations.

22

Conflict Resolution Strategies

Conflict is an inevitable part of life, and this chapter delves into strategies for resolving conflicts when they do arise. Topics explored include:

Mediation and Resolution Techniques: Learn about mediation and other conflict resolution techniques that can be applied to a wide range of disputes, whether personal or professional.

Effective Communication in Conflict: Understand the principles of effective communication during conflict, including active listening and the use of nonviolent communication.

Effective conflict resolution strategies are essential for addressing conflicts, disputes, and disagreements while considering the psychological aspects of those involved. In the context of "Understanding the Enemy: Psychology in Conflict," it's crucial to adopt strategies that take into account the motivations, emotions, and perceptions of individuals or groups in conflict. Here, we explore conflict resolution strategies with a focus on their psychological perspective:

Active Listening and Empathy: Actively listening to the concerns and viewpoints of all parties is fundamental. Empathizing with their emotions and perspectives fosters understanding and trust. This psychological approach creates an environment where individuals feel heard and validated, making them more open to resolution.

Communication Skills: Effective communication is the cornerstone of conflict resolution. Psychologically sensitive communication involves clear and assertive expression of one's own needs and concerns, combined with the ability to use non-confrontational language and actively address the emotional dimensions of the conflict.

Mediation: A neutral mediator can facilitate dialogue and guide parties in understanding each other's viewpoints. Mediators use their psychological insight to help participants find common ground and encourage productive discussion.

Conflict Analysis: Delve into the motivations and underlying causes of the conflict. By analyzing the psychological factors at play, you can tailor your strategies to address the root issues and not just the surface-level disagreements.

Conflict Resolution Styles: Different conflict resolution styles, such as collaboration, compromise, avoidance, accommodation, or competition, can be applied depending on the psychological dynamics of the conflict. A psychologically attuned approach considers which style is most appropriate for the situation.

Emotional Intelligence: Developing emotional intelligence is crucial in understanding the psychological aspects of conflict. Emotionally intelligent individuals can navigate and manage their emotions and empathize with the emotions of others, leading to more effective conflict resolution.

Trauma-Informed Approaches: In conflicts that involve trauma, a trauma-informed approach considers the psychological well-being of individuals. It involves creating a safe and supportive environment for those affected by trauma and addressing their unique needs.

Cultural Sensitivity: Cultural awareness and sensitivity are essential when dealing with conflicts involving diverse groups. Understanding cultural nuances and respecting cultural differences can be key to successful conflict resolution.

Conflict Prevention: Preventing conflicts from escalating often requires a psychological perspective that recognizes early signs and triggers. By addressing potential issues at an early stage, you can avert more significant conflicts.

Long-Term Resolution: A psychological approach to conflict resolution also considers the long-term well-being of those involved. Strategies aim for sustainable solutions that address not only the immediate issues but also the psychological and emotional recovery of all parties.

Incorporating these psychological perspectives into conflict resolution strategies promotes more empathetic, effective, and lasting resolutions. It acknowledges the complexity of human emotions, motivations, and perceptions in conflicts, ultimately contributing to a more peaceful and harmonious environment.

139

23

Building Win-Win Solutions

The ultimate aim of conflict resolution and negotiation is to achieve win-win solutions, where all parties benefit. In this chapter, you'll delve into the strategies for crafting agreements that lead to mutual success:

Collaborative Problem-Solving: Explore collaborative problem-solving techniques that enable conflicting parties to work together in finding creative and beneficial solutions.

The Art of Compromise: Understand the importance of compromise and how to find middle ground in conflicts to create outcomes that satisfy all parties involved.

Part V offers a comprehensive guide to conflict resolution and negotiation, leveraging the wisdom derived from the art of warfare and diplomacy. By embracing diplomacy and negotiation to avoid unnecessary battles, understanding the psychology of conflict, mastering conflict resolution strategies, and striving for win-win solutions, you equip yourself with the skills to navigate conflicts effectively, preserve relationships, and achieve mutually beneficial resolutions in various facets of your life.

Conflict resolution and negotiation are fundamental skills that play a crucial role in both personal and professional life. Here are some key facts about conflict resolution and negotiation:

Prevention is the Best Approach: Effective conflict resolution often begins with conflict prevention. By fostering open communication, setting clear expectations, and addressing issues proactively, many conflicts can be avoided altogether.

The Win-Win Approach: The best conflict resolutions result in win-win outcomes, where all parties involved benefit. This approach is more sustainable and conducive to maintaining positive relationships.

Active Listening: Active listening is a cornerstone of successful negotiation and conflict resolution. It involves not only hearing the words of the other party but also understanding their perspective, feelings, and underlying needs.

Conflict Can Lead to Innovation: Some conflicts, if managed and resolved effectively, can lead to innovation and positive change. Differing viewpoints can be sources of creativity and progress.

Mediation is Valuable: In many conflicts, a neutral third party, such as a mediator, can be highly effective in facilitating resolution. Mediators can help guide discussions, maintain neutrality, and ensure that all parties have a voice in the process.

Emotions Play a Significant Role: Emotions are often at the heart of conflicts, and understanding and managing emotional responses is critical to successful resolution. Emotionally intelligent negotiation can lead to more constructive outcomes.

Cultural Awareness is Important: Culture plays a significant role in conflict resolution and negotiation. Different cultures may have varying approaches to conflict, communication styles, and expectations for resolution.

Conflict Resolution Skills are Transferable: Conflict resolution and negotiation skills are not limited to resolving disputes; they are transferable skills that can be applied to various aspects of life, including problem-solving, decision-making, and relationship-building.

Power Imbalance Matters: In some conflicts, there may be a significant power imbalance between parties. Negotiators and mediators must be aware of these imbalances and work to ensure that all parties are treated fairly.

Consensus-Building: Effective negotiation often involves consensus-building, where all parties agree on a solution. Consensus can be more durable and lead to greater commitment to the agreed-upon terms.

Long-Term vs. Short-Term Solutions: Conflict resolution strategies can vary in their focus on short-term or long-term solutions. Depending on the situation, the emphasis may be on resolving the immediate issue or addressing underlying systemic problems.

Legal Implications: In some cases, conflicts have legal implications, and negotiation may lead to legally binding agreements. Legal professionals, such as lawyers and arbitrators, may be involved in these cases.

Training and Skill Development: Conflict resolution and negotiation skills can be developed and improved through training, education, and practice. Many organizations offer conflict resolution training to employees.

Online and International Negotiations: In our increasingly globalized world, negotiations can occur online and across international borders. These contexts introduce additional challenges related to technology, language, and cross-cultural communication.

Negotiation Styles: People have different negotiation styles. Some may be competitive, seeking to maximize their own gain, while others may be more collaborative, prioritizing mutually beneficial solutions. Understanding and adapting to these styles is crucial for successful negotiation.

Conflict resolution and negotiation are invaluable skills that contribute to effective communication, relationship management, and problem-solving. Whether in personal relationships, business transactions, or international diplomacy, these skills are essential for achieving peaceful, constructive, and mutually beneficial outcomes.

Conflict resolution and negotiation come with their own set of advantages and disadvantages, which can vary depending on the context, the individuals involved, and the specific methods employed. Here's an overview of these pros and cons:

Advantages of Conflict Resolution and Negotiation:

Conflict Prevention: Early conflict resolution and negotiation can prevent conflicts from escalating into more serious and destructive disputes.

Maintaining Relationships: Effective conflict resolution and negotiation can preserve and even strengthen relationships. When handled well, they can prevent irreparable damage to personal or professional connections.

Win-Win Outcomes: Negotiation often aims for win-win solutions, where all parties involved benefit. This can lead to a more sustainable and harmonious result.

Creativity and Innovation: Conflict resolution and negotiation can stimulate creativity and innovation as individuals bring different perspectives and ideas to the table.

Empowerment: By giving all parties a voice in the process, conflict resolution and negotiation empower individuals to have a say in the outcome, which can enhance their sense of control and satisfaction.

Increased Communication Skills: Conflict resolution and negotiation require effective communication, which can lead to improved communication skills in general.

Efficient Problem-Solving: These processes are effective for solving problems and addressing issues, which is valuable in various aspects of life, including work, family, and community interactions.

Lower Costs: In some cases, resolving conflicts through negotiation can be less costly and time-consuming than pursuing litigation or adversarial approaches.

Disadvantages of Conflict Resolution and Negotiation:

No Guarantee of Resolution: Not all conflicts can be successfully resolved through negotiation. There's no guarantee that all parties will come to an agreement, and this can lead to ongoing disputes.

Time-Consuming: Conflict resolution and negotiation can be time-consuming, especially when multiple parties are involved and when disputes are complex.

Emotional Strain: Conflict and negotiation can be emotionally taxing, especially in personal disputes. Handling intense emotions can be challenging.
Unequal Power Dynamics: In situations with significant power imbalances, negotiation may not lead to fair outcomes. The stronger party may dominate the process.

Cultural and Communication Challenges: Cross-cultural negotiations can be challenging due to differences in communication styles, customs, and expectations.

Risk of Compromise: In some cases, negotiation may lead to compromises that aren't truly satisfactory for any party, potentially leaving everyone feeling dissatisfied.

Legal Implications: In conflicts with legal ramifications, negotiation may not resolve all legal issues, leading to potential legal consequences later on.

Mediation and Facilitation Costs: When third-party mediators or facilitators are involved, there may be additional costs associated with their services.

It's essential to recognize that conflict resolution and negotiation are not one-size-fits-all solutions. Their success and applicability depend on the specific circumstances and the willingness of parties to engage in the process. In many cases, the advantages, such as preserving relationships and achieving win-win outcomes, far outweigh the disadvantages. However, it's important to be aware of the limitations and potential challenges associated with these approaches

VI

Personal Development

The journey of life is not merely about external achievements but also about inner growth and self-improvement. Part VI focuses on personal development, drawing from the wisdom of the principles of war to empower individuals to enhance their skills, knowledge, and character.

24

A Path to Self-Realization and Growth

Personal development is a lifelong journey that involves the continuous enhancement of one's skills, knowledge, qualities, and experiences. It aims to foster self-realization and personal growth, helping individuals become the best versions of themselves. Let's explore personal development in greater detail based on the title's theme:

Self-Realization: Personal development begins with self-realization. It's the process of gaining a deep understanding of who you are, what you value, and what you want to achieve. Self-awareness is the foundation upon which personal development is built.

Setting Goals: Setting clear, meaningful goals is a fundamental aspect of personal development. These goals guide your efforts, provide direction, and serve as a source of motivation. They can encompass various aspects of life, including career, relationships, health, and personal growth.

Lifelong Learning: Personal development embraces the concept of lifelong learning. This involves continually acquiring new knowledge, skills, and experiences to expand your horizons and remain adaptable in an ever-changing world.

Self-Improvement: Self-improvement is at the core of personal development. It includes areas like enhancing your communication skills, increasing emotional intelligence, and honing your problem-solving abilities.

Emotional Intelligence: Understanding and managing your emotions, as well as recognizing and empathizing with the emotions of others, is a crucial part of personal development. Emotional intelligence is vital for building positive relationships and navigating social interactions effectively.

Time Management: Effective time management is integral to personal development. It helps individuals make the most of their time, prioritize tasks, and maintain a work-life balance.

Mindfulness and Self-Care: Incorporating mindfulness and self-care practices into personal development can enhance mental well-being. These practices promote stress reduction, emotional regulation, and self-compassion.

Self-Confidence: Building self-confidence is essential for personal development. It involves recognizing your strengths and abilities and embracing a positive self-image.

Leadership Skills: Developing leadership skills, even if you don't hold a leadership position, is valuable. These skills encompass effective communication, decision-making, and the ability to influence and motivate others.

Interpersonal Skills: Personal development places a significant emphasis on enhancing interpersonal skills. This includes building effective relationships, resolving conflicts, and developing empathy.

Networking: Networking is an essential element of personal development, as it enables you to connect with individuals who can provide support, mentorship, and opportunities for growth.

Financial Literacy: Understanding personal finances and financial planning is another facet of personal development. This knowledge empowers individuals to make informed decisions about their financial well-being.

Health and Well-being: Personal development includes a focus on physical and mental health. Taking care of your physical health, exercise, and adopting a healthy lifestyle contributes to personal growth.

Reflection and Goal Adjustment: Personal development is an iterative process. Regularly reflecting on your progress, adjusting your goals, and reassessing your priorities are essential to staying on track and evolving.

In conclusion, personal development is a transformative journey that encompasses self-awareness, goal setting, continuous learning, and self-improvement. It's a path to self-realization and personal growth, helping individuals become more capable, confident, and fulfilled in various aspects of their lives.

25

Self-Improvement and Continuous Learning

In this chapter, we explore the inexhaustible pursuit of self-improvement and continuous learning. Just as soldiers hone their skills and adapt to new challenges, you'll discover how to cultivate a growth mindset, embrace lifelong learning, and nurture personal development throughout your life. In the context of personal development, self-improvement and continuous learning serve as foundational pillars, driving individuals toward self-realization and growth. Let's delve into these crucial aspects of personal development:

Self-Improvement - The Ongoing Journey: Self-improvement is the ongoing process of enhancing one's knowledge, skills, and qualities. It encompasses a commitment to becoming the best version of oneself and achieving personal excellence.

Goal Setting: Self-improvement often begins with setting clear, achievable goals. These goals provide direction and motivation for the journey of personal growth.

Self-Awareness: Self-improvement is built upon self-awareness. It involves recognizing your strengths and weaknesses, understanding your values, and identifying areas where you wish to improve.

Embracing Challenges: To grow, individuals must embrace challenges and step out of their comfort zones. These challenges may include acquiring new skills, taking on new responsibilities, or confronting personal fears.

Adaptability: Self-improvement requires adaptability. It means being open to change and having a growth mindset, which is the belief that abilities and intelligence can be developed over time through effort and learning.

Continuous Learning – The Lifelong Pursuit: Continuous learning is the practice of acquiring new knowledge and skills throughout one's life. It supports self-improvement by expanding one's horizons and enabling individuals to adapt to an ever-evolving world.

Formal and Informal Education: Continuous learning can take various forms, including formal education, online courses, workshops, seminars, and informal self-study.

Open-Mindedness: A key aspect of continuous learning is open-mindedness. It involves being receptive to new ideas, perspectives, and experiences.

Problem-Solving: Learning often involves problem-solving. Individuals acquire new skills and knowledge to solve real-world problems and challenges effectively.

Broadening Horizons: Continuous learning broadens one's horizons, providing exposure to different cultures, fields, and viewpoints. This broader perspective can be instrumental in personal development.

Staying Current: In a rapidly changing world, continuous learning helps individuals stay current and relevant in their chosen fields, whether professionally or personally.

Self-improvement and continuous learning are interconnected and mutually reinforcing. Self-improvement drives individuals to seek new knowledge and skills, while continuous learning supports self-improvement by providing the tools and resources for growth.

Together, they form a dynamic cycle of personal development, enabling individuals to adapt, excel, and continually evolve. These pillars empower individuals to lead more fulfilling lives and make valuable contributions to society by fostering self-awareness, adaptability, and a commitment to lifelong learning.

26

Harnessing Creativity and Innovation

Creativity and innovation are the driving forces of progress, whether on the battlefield or in the realm of ideas. Chapter 26 delves into the art of nurturing creativity and innovation, offering techniques to spark ingenuity, overcome mental barriers, and unleash your creative potential.

Creativity and innovation are dynamic forces that drive progress and shape the future. In the context of personal development, these capabilities play a significant role in fostering growth, problem-solving, and self-realization. Let's explore the importance and facets of harnessing creativity and innovation:

Importance of Creativity and Innovation:

Problem-Solving: Creativity and innovation are at the heart of effective problem-solving. They allow individuals to think beyond conventional solutions, devising novel approaches to challenges.

Continuous Learning: Embracing creativity and innovation encourages continuous learning. It prompts individuals to seek new knowledge, experiment, and adapt to changing circumstances.

Personal Growth: Harnessing these qualities fosters personal growth by pushing individuals to expand their horizons, take risks, and discover their capabilities.

Professional Success: In the professional realm, creativity and innovation are highly valued. They can lead to career advancement, entrepreneurship, and the development of groundbreaking products and services.

Adaptability: In a rapidly changing world, creativity and innovation enable individuals to adapt to new situations and seize opportunities.

Harnessing Creativity:

Open-Mindedness: Open-mindedness is a key aspect of harnessing creativity. It involves being receptive to new ideas, perspectives, and experiences, which can stimulate creative thinking.

Curiosity: Cultivating curiosity fuels creativity. It prompts individuals to explore, ask questions, and seek solutions beyond the obvious.

Divergent Thinking: Creativity often involves divergent thinking, which is the ability to generate a multitude of ideas and solutions. It encourages thinking "outside the box."

Risk-Taking: Creativity may require taking calculated risks. A willingness to step out of one's comfort zone can lead to innovative breakthroughs.

Expression: Various forms of creative expression, such as art, writing, or music, provide outlets for creativity and self–discovery.

Harnessing Innovation:

Identifying Opportunities: Innovation begins with identifying opportunities for improvement or new ideas. It requires a keen awareness of unmet needs or areas with potential for growth.

Collaboration: Collaborative innovation involves working with others to generate and implement ideas. It leverages the collective creativity of a group.

Adaptability: Innovation often requires adaptability. Individuals must be willing to adjust their approaches and pivot based on feedback and changing circumstances.

Problem Definition: Clearly defining the problem or challenge is essential for effective innovation. A well-defined problem leads to targeted, meaningful solutions.

Prototyping and Testing: Innovators frequently engage in prototyping and testing to refine their ideas. This iterative process helps identify flaws and improve solutions.

Harnessing creativity and innovation in personal development empowers individuals to break through barriers, discover new opportunities, and continuously evolve. By fostering a culture of curiosity, open-mindedness, and risk-taking, individuals can channel their creative energies to make meaningful contributions to their personal and professional lives. Whether through artistic expression, problem-solving, or entrepreneurial endeavors, creativity and innovation are catalysts for growth and self-realization.

27

Resourcefulness and Problem-Solving

Resourcefulness, a quality revered in military leaders, is invaluable in navigating the complexities of life. This chapter delves into the art of resourcefulness and problem-solving, providing insights into finding solutions, making the most of available resources, and overcoming obstacles with creativity and resilience.

Resourcefulness and problem-solving are essential skills that empower individuals to overcome challenges, seize opportunities, and drive personal development. Let's explore these skills in the context of personal growth:

Importance of Resourcefulness and Problem-Solving:

Adaptability: Resourcefulness and problem-solving enable individuals to adapt to changing circumstances and navigate unexpected obstacles effectively.

Self-Reliance: Resourcefulness encourages self-reliance and self-confidence. It empowers individuals to find solutions independently, fostering a sense of autonomy.

Innovation: Resourcefulness often involves innovative thinking, which can lead to creative solutions and novel approaches to challenges.

Effective Decision-Making: Problem-solving is closely linked to decision-making. It enables individuals to make informed choices when faced with complex situations.

Resilience: The ability to solve problems and find resources when needed enhances resilience, helping individuals bounce back from setbacks.

Resourcefulness:

Creative Problem-Solving: Resourcefulness often involves creative problem-solving. It means thinking beyond conventional solutions and finding alternative paths to achieve goals.

Optimizing Available Resources: Resourceful individuals make the most of the resources at their disposal, whether those are financial, informational, or social.

Networking: Building a strong network and knowing how to leverage it is a resourceful skill. It allows individuals to access knowledge, support, and opportunities.

Adaptability: Resourcefulness involves being adaptable and open to new ideas and methods. It's about continuously seeking ways to improve and overcome challenges.

Self-Efficacy: Believing in one's ability to find solutions and adapt to changing situations is a core aspect of resourcefulness.

Problem-Solving:

Analytical Thinking: Problem-solving often involves analytical thinking, where individuals break down complex issues into manageable components to identify potential solutions.

Critical Thinking: Critical thinking is the ability to evaluate information, arguments, and situations objectively and make informed judgments.

Decision-Making: Problem-solving and decision-making go hand in hand. Effective decision-making involves weighing pros and cons, considering consequences, and choosing the best course of action.

Systematic Approach: A systematic approach to problem-solving involves defining the problem, generating potential solutions, evaluating those solutions, and implementing the best one.

Learning from Failure: Problem-solving also includes the ability to learn from failure. It's about seeing setbacks as opportunities for growth and improvement.

Resourcefulness and problem-solving are complementary skills that empower individuals to address challenges and seize opportunities in their personal and professional lives. By fostering these skills, individuals can build a strong foundation for personal development, enabling them to navigate a world filled with complexities and uncertainties. Resourcefulness allows them to maximize available resources, while problem-solving equips them with the tools to overcome obstacles and make effective decisions. Together, these skills contribute to resilience, adaptability, and continuous growth.

28

The Path to Mastery

Mastery is the culmination of dedication and unwavering commitment to a skill or field. Drawing from the principles of war, this chapter explores the path to mastery. It reveals the stages of skill development, the importance of deliberate practice, and the enduring journey toward excellence in any chosen pursuit.

In Part VI, we embark on a quest of personal development, embodying the spirit of growth, creativity, resourcefulness, and mastery. By embracing these principles and applying them to your life, you can continually evolve and refine your skills, expand your knowledge, and cultivate a character rooted in wisdom and resilience. This section serves as a guide to personal transformation, empowering you to thrive and excel in the ever-evolving landscape of existence.

Reasons for Personal Development:

Self-Improvement: Personal development is an ongoing journey of self-improvement, allowing individuals to become the best versions of themselves. It helps you refine your skills, expand your knowledge, and cultivate positive traits.

Career Advancement: Personal development often leads to enhanced job performance and career advancement. By acquiring new skills and knowledge, you can become more valuable in the workplace and open up new opportunities.

Life Fulfillment: Personal development can contribute to a sense of fulfillment and happiness. Achieving goals, growing as an individual, and realizing your potential can be deeply satisfying.

Increased Confidence: As you develop your skills and knowledge, your confidence grows. This newfound self-assureds can have a positive impact on various aspects of your life.

Adaptability: In a rapidly changing world, personal development equips you with the adaptability to thrive in evolving circumstances. It prepares you to face new challenges and embrace change with confidence.

Goal Achievement: Personal development provides you with the tools and motivation to set and achieve goals. It allows you to plan and work toward your objectives more effectively.

Obstacles behind Personal Development:

Lack of Time: Many people feel they have limited time for personal development due to work, family, and other commitments. Finding time for self-improvement can be challenging.

Resistance to Change: Personal development often requires stepping out of your comfort zone, which can be uncomfortable and met with resistance. Fear of change can hinder progress.

Procrastination: Procrastination is a common obstacle. Putting off tasks related to personal development can impede growth and goal achievement.

Lack of Direction: Without clear goals and a well-defined plan, personal development efforts may lack focus and direction. Uncertainty about what to pursue can be a barrier.

Financial Constraints: Some forms of personal development, such as education and training, can be costly. Financial limitations may prevent access to certain opportunities

Negative Self-Beliefs: Low self-esteem and self-doubt can hinder personal development efforts. Believing that you are not capable of improvement can be a significant obstacle.

Overwhelming Choices: The vast array of self-help resources and options for personal development can be overwhelming. People may struggle to choose the most suitable path.

Lack of Support: A lack of support or encouragement from friends, family, or mentors can make personal development efforts more challenging. A supportive network can provide motivation and guidance.

Burnout: Pushing too hard for personal development without proper rest and self-care can lead to burnout, which hampers progress.

Fear of Failure: The fear of failing in personal development efforts can be paralyzing. The possibility of not achieving desired outcomes can deter individuals from taking action.

Overcoming these obstacles often requires a combination of self-awareness, goal-setting, time management, perseverance, and seeking support. It's important to recognize that obstacles are a natural part of the personal development journey, and with determination and the right strategies, they can be navigated and overcome.

VII

Success in the Modern World

In the fast-paced and ever-evolving landscape of the modern world, success takes on new dimensions. Part VII delves into the principles that underpin success in the digital age, drawing inspiration from the strategic insights of war and applying them to the challenges of contemporary life.

29

Success in the Modern World: Navigating Challenges and Seizing Opportunities

Success in the modern world is a dynamic and multifaceted concept, shaped by a rapidly evolving global landscape. Achieving success in the modern era requires adaptability, innovation, and a keen awareness of the challenges and opportunities that this ever-changing world presents. Here's a deeper exploration of success in the modern world:

Defining Success: Modern success is often defined by a broader perspective that goes beyond traditional measures like financial wealth or career achievements. It includes personal fulfillment, a balanced lifestyle, and making a positive impact on society.

Embracing Change: The modern world is characterized by constant change, driven by technological advancements and global shifts. Success involves the ability to adapt to change and thrive in dynamic environments.

Continuous Learning: Lifelong learning is a cornerstone of modern success. Embracing new knowledge and skills is essential to stay relevant in a world where information and technology evolve rapidly.

Innovation and Creativity: Success in the modern world often hinges on innovation and creativity. These qualities drive new solutions, business ventures, and social change.

Tech Proficiency: Proficiency with technology is a vital skill for success in the modern world. Being tech-savvy is not limited to IT professionals; it's a fundamental skill for various industries and daily life.

Global Awareness: The modern world is interconnected. Success requires an understanding of global trends, cross-cultural competence, and the ability to work with diverse individuals and teams

Problem-Solving and Critical Thinking: Modern success relies on the ability to solve complex problems and think critically. These skills are essential in various fields, from business to healthcare.

Adaptability: Success means being adaptable and resilient in the face of uncertainty and change. Adaptability enables individuals to pivot, learn, and grow in the midst of challenges.

Digital Literacy: Proficiency in navigating digital platforms, data analysis, and understanding digital trends are key components of success in the digital age.

Entrepreneurship and Innovation: Entrepreneurs who harness innovative thinking and take calculated risks often drive modern success stories. Start-ups and innovative ventures thrive in this environment.

Work-Life Balance: Modern success acknowledges the importance of work-life balance and mental well-being. A healthy, balanced life contributes to long-term success and personal fulfillment.

Environmental Awareness: A commitment to environmental sustainability and ethical practices is increasingly part of modern success. Individuals and organizations that prioritize these values are seen as successful.

Leadership and Social Impact: Success often includes leadership and making a positive impact on society. Leaders who inspire change and social betterment are considered successful in the modern world.

Personal Growth and Self-Realization: Success also involves personal growth and self-realization. It's about becoming the best version of oneself and living a life aligned with one's values and aspirations.

Success in the modern world is a multifaceted journey, incorporating professional achievement, personal growth, and social responsibility. It's about embracing change, staying adaptable, and pursuing continuous learning and innovation. Success in this context is a holistic concept that recognizes the interplay between personal and professional aspects of life and the impact one can have on the broader world.

30

Technology and Information Warfare

In the digital era, technology and information are the new battlegrounds. This chapter explores the strategies for mastering these domains, from harnessing the power of technology to waging effective information warfare. It emphasizes the importance of digital literacy and the ability to navigate the digital realm. In the modern world, the strategic use of technology and information is a crucial element of success. As part of the 33 successful tactics for navigating contemporary challenges, the effective utilization of technology and information warfare plays a vital role. Let's delve into this concept and explore how it contributes to success:

Information Warfare Tactics:

Information warfare tactics play a critical role in shaping public perception, influencing decision-making, and achieving strategic goals. Whether you're an individual seeking to protect your online presence or an organization aiming to establish a strong digital reputation, understanding and utilizing information warfare tactics is vital. Here are key aspects of information warfare tactics:

Cyber security: Protecting digital assets and information is paramount. Successful individuals and organizations employ robust cyber security measures to safeguard sensitive data and maintain trust

Data Analytics: Harnessing the power of data analytics enables individuals and organizations to gain insights, make informed decisions, and stay ahead in various fields.

Media Literacy: In a world filled with information, success requires media literacy. This skill helps in discerning credible sources from misinformation and disinformation.

Strategic Communication: Effective communication is key in information warfare. Crafting and delivering messages that align with goals and values are a vital tactic.

Online Reputation Management: Maintaining a positive online presence is essential. Individuals and businesses use online reputation management strategies to shape public perception.

Technology Integration: Technology integration is a critical component of achieving success and maintaining relevance in various fields. This process involves the seamless incorporation of technology into daily activities, processes, and strategies.

Innovation Ecosystems: Successful entities create innovation ecosystems that foster creativity, collaboration, and the development of cutting-edge technologies.

Automation and AI: Automation and artificial intelligence are harnessed to enhance efficiency and productivity, reducing mundane tasks and freeing up time for strategic thinking.

Cloud Computing: Cloud technologies provide scalability and flexibility, enabling businesses to adapt quickly to changing demands.

IOT (Internet of Things): The IOT is leveraged to collect and analyze data from interconnected devices, improving decision-making and enhancing user experiences.

Blockchain: Blockchain technology is employed for secure transactions, supply chain management, and ensuring the integrity of data.

Social Media and Online Presence:
In the contemporary world, a strong online presence and effective use of social media are integral

components of personal and professional success. They allow individuals and organizations to connect with a global audience, build relationships, and influence outcomes. Let's explore the significance and strategies for leveraging social media and cultivating a strong online presence:

Digital Marketing: Leveraging digital marketing strategies on social media platforms to reach and engage with a global audience is a fundamental tactic for success.

Personal Branding: Individuals build strong personal brands through social media, enabling them to connect with opportunities and like-minded individuals.

Content Creation: Creating high-quality, relevant content is essential for maintaining an online presence and building an audience.

Online Networking: Successful networking extends beyond traditional means, encompassing online platforms for global connections and opportunities.

Geopolitical and Security Considerations:

Geopolitical and security considerations are vital for ensuring personal and professional success. Understanding global dynamics, assessing risks, and implementing security measures are crucial for individuals and organizations alike. Let's delve into the significance and strategies related to geopolitical and security considerations:

Geopolitical Analysis: Understanding the geopolitical landscape helps individuals and organizations make informed decisions and mitigate risks.

Security Protocols: Employing robust security protocols, both online and offline, safeguards assets and information.

31

Cyber security and Defense: Protecting Your Life

The digital world is not without its threats. This chapter delves into the critical importance of cyber security and defense, highlighting the strategies for protecting your personal and professional life from cyber threats and vulnerabilities.

cybersecurity and defense are paramount for preserving your personal and professional well-being. Protecting your life in the digital realm involves a range of measures and strategies:

Significance of Cybersecurity and Defense:

Personal Privacy: Cybersecurity measures are essential to maintain the privacy of your personal information and protect against unauthorized access.

Financial Security: Safeguarding your financial data and online transactions is crucial for preventing fraud, identity theft, and financial losses.

Reputation Management: Effective cybersecurity is key to maintaining a positive online reputation by preventing cyber attacks and mitigating online threats.

Digital Assets: Protecting digital assets, such as important documents, photos, and other digital property, ensures their integrity and availability.

Professional Success: In the professional realm, cybersecurity is fundamental for safeguarding sensitive business information, trade secrets, and customer data, as a security breach can have severe consequences for your career or business.

Key Strategies for Cybersecurity and Defense:

Strong Passwords: Create complex, unique passwords for online accounts, and consider using a reputable password manager to assist in password management.

Two-Factor Authentication (2FA): Enable 2FA wherever possible to add an extra layer of security to your accounts.

Regular Updates: Keep your operating system, software, and security programs up to date to patch vulnerabilities and protect against known threats.
Secure Wi-Fi: Protect your home network with a strong, unique password and enable encryption to prevent unauthorized access.

Phishing Awareness: Stay cautious of phishing attempts and suspicious emails, verifying the sender's authenticity before clicking on links or providing personal information.

Firewalls and Antivirus Software: Install and regularly update firewalls and antivirus software to protect against malware and cyber threats.

Data Backups: Regularly back up your data to an external source or cloud storage to ensure you can recover it in case of data loss or a cyber incident.

Privacy Settings: Review and adjust the privacy settings on your social media accounts and other online platforms to control who can access your information.

Cyber Hygiene: Practice good cyber hygiene by being cautious with downloads, avoiding public Wi-Fi for sensitive transactions, and monitoring your digital presence.

Education and Awareness:

Stay informed about the latest cyber threats, scams, and security best practices through reputable sources and remain vigilant.

Educate yourself and your family about the importance of cybersecurity and the potential risks associated with online activities.

Keep up with security updates and consider cybersecurity training or courses to enhance your knowledge and skills.

Professional Assistance:

For complex security needs, consider consulting with cybersecurity professionals or hiring them to assess and enhance your digital security. moreso For businesses, employ cybersecurity experts or services to ensure the protection of sensitive data and customer information.

Cybersecurity and defense are critical for protecting your personal and professional life in the digital age. By implementing robust security practices and staying informed about potential threats, you can reduce the risk of cyber incidents and enjoy the benefits of a secure digital existence. This not only preserves your personal information but also contributes to your overall success and peace of mind in the modern world.

32

Economic Strategies: Accumulating Wealth

Economic success is a central pursuit in the modern world. Chapter 32 delves into economic strategies, from financial planning and investment to wealth accumulation. It offers insights into managing resources wisely and making informed financial decisions. Accumulating wealth is a goal that many individuals aspire to achieve, and it involves a combination of financial planning, investment, and prudent economic strategies. Here are key strategies for accumulating wealth:

Financial Planning:

Financial planning is an ongoing process that adapts to changes in your life and economic circumstances. It helps you achieve your financial goals, build wealth, and secure a financially stable future. By following these key principles, you can navigate the complexities of personal finance and work toward your financial objectives.

Budgeting: Create a detailed budget to track your income and expenses. This will help you identify areas where you can save and invest.

Emergency Fund: Establish an emergency fund with at least three to six months' worth of living expenses.

This safety net ensures you're financially prepared for unexpected events.

Debt Management: Prioritize paying off high-interest debt, such as credit card debt, to free up more of your income for saving and investing.

Savings Goals: Set specific savings goals, whether it's for a down payment on a house, retirement, or other financial objectives.

Investing:

Investing is a dynamic and rewarding way to build wealth over time, but it requires careful planning, risk management, and informed decision-making. By following these principles and staying committed to your investment strategy, you can work toward achieving your financial objectives and securing your financial future.

Diversification: Diversify your investment portfolio to spread risk. Invest in a mix of assets, such as stocks, bonds, real estate, and mutual funds.

Long-Term Perspective: Adopt a long-term investment approach. Compound interest can significantly grow your wealth over time.

Automatic Contributions: Set up automatic contributions to your investment accounts to ensure consistent savings and investments.

Professional Advice: Consider seeking advice from a financial advisor or investment professional to make informed decisions.

Income Generation:

Increasing your income is a fundamental part of achieving financial security and building wealth. Here are strategies to boost your earnings:

Career Growth: Focus on career development and seek opportunities for promotions and salary increases.

Multiple Income Streams: Explore opportunities for additional income, such as a side business, freelance work, or investments that generate passive income.

Tax Efficiency:

Tax efficiency involves structuring your finances and investments to minimize your tax liability while legally taking advantage of tax benefits. Here are key strategies to enhance your tax efficiency:

Tax-Advantaged Accounts: Take advantage of tax-advantaged accounts, like 401(k)s, IRAs, and HSAs, to minimize tax liability and maximize savings.

Tax Planning: Understand tax strategies and consult with a tax professional to optimize your tax situation.

Frugality and Cost Savings:

Frugality and cost savings involve making conscious, efficient choices to manage your expenses and improve your financial well-being. Here are key strategies for embracing frugality and saving money:

Live Below Your Means: Avoid unnecessary expenses and maintain a lifestyle that is below your income level. Save or invest the difference.

Negotiation: Negotiate for better deals and discounts whenever possible, whether it's for a major purchase or everyday expenses.

Continuous Learning:

Continuous learning, also known as lifelong learning, is the practice of acquiring new knowledge, skills, and experiences throughout your life. It is an essential element for personal and professional growth. Here's how you can embrace continuous learning:

Financial Literacy: Invest in your financial education. The more you understand about personal finance and investing, the better equipped you'll be to make sound decisions.

Risk Management:

Risk management involves identifying, assessing, and mitigating potential threats and uncertainties that can impact your financial well-being and personal life. Here's how you can effectively manage risk:

Insurance: Protect your assets and wealth with appropriate insurance coverage, including health, life, and property insurance.

Estate Planning: Establish a will and estate plan to ensure the orderly transfer of your wealth to heirs or beneficiaries.

Networking and Collaboration:

Networking: Build relationships with individuals who have expertise in finance and investing. They can offer valuable insights and opportunities.

Partnerships: Consider partnerships or collaborations that can amplify your wealth-building efforts, such as real estate investments with others.

Philanthropy and Giving:

Charitable Giving: Consider incorporating philanthropy into your wealth accumulation strategy. Giving back can be personally fulfilling and may also provide tax benefits.

Review and Adjust:

Regularly review your financial goals and progress. Adjust your strategies as your circumstances change or as you get closer to your goals.

Accumulating wealth is a long-term endeavor that requires discipline, patience, and strategic planning. By implementing these economic strategies and staying committed to your financial goals, you can work toward building and preserving your wealth over time.

33

The Ever-Changing Landscape: Adapting to the Digital Age

The digital age is characterized by constant change. This chapter focuses on the adaptability required to thrive in an ever-evolving landscape. It highlights the importance of staying agile, embracing change, and leveraging technology to navigate the challenges and opportunities of the modern world.

In Part VII, we step into the heart of success in the contemporary world, where technology, information, economics, and adaptability are key players. By drawing inspiration from the principles of war and applying them to these digital domains, you can equip yourself to navigate the complexities of the modern world, safeguard your digital life, and pursue economic success while maintaining the agility required thriving in a rapidly changing environment. This section serves as a guide to achieving success in an era where digital literacy and adaptability are essential skills.

Success in the Modern World

In the journey through "Success in the Modern World," we've explored the multifaceted facets of achieving prosperity and fulfillment in the ever-evolving landscape of the digital age. Drawing inspiration from military strategies, this section has shed light on essential principles and domains that underpin contemporary success.

Technology and Information Warfare: In the digital era, harnessing the power of technology and mastering the art of information warfare are paramount. Success involves digital literacy and the ability to navigate the digital realm effectively.

Cyber security and Defense: Protecting one's personal and professional life from cyber threats and vulnerabilities is essential. This chapter emphasized the significance of cyber security in the modern world.

Economic Strategies: Managing resources wisely, making informed financial decisions, and working towards wealth accumulation are key components of success in the economic domain.

Adaptability to Change: The modern world is characterized by constant change. Success requires adaptability, embracing change, and leveraging technology to navigate the challenges and opportunities of the digital age

In conclusion, "Success in the Modern World" is a dynamic and ever-relevant pursuit, demanding a keen understanding of technology, the ability to protect one's digital life, astute economic strategies, and above all, adaptability in the face of rapid change. These principles drawn from the strategies of war provide a blueprint for thriving in the complexities of the contemporary landscape. Success in the modern world is not a fixed destination but a journey, requiring a combination of knowledge, resilience, and agility to excel in the digital age.

Conclusion

The application of above title "33 Life Success Tactics Rooted in the Principles of War" holds relevance and applicability to the global world in a multitude of ways. Here's how this approach can be applied on a broader scale:

Leadership and Diplomacy: The principles of leadership and diplomacy discussed in the book can be extended to the global stage. International leaders can benefit from understanding effective leadership, negotiation, and diplomacy, which are essential in fostering cooperation, resolving conflicts, and addressing global issues.

Strategic Thinking for Global Challenges: Global issues such as climate change, pandemics, and economic crises require strategic thinking. Applying the principles of war, including long-term planning, adaptability, and considering the broader implications of actions, can aid in addressing these challenges effectively.

International Relations and Conflict Resolution: The book's insights into conflict resolution and negotiation are highly relevant to international relations. Diplomats and negotiators can benefit from these strategies when working on complex global conflicts and peace-building efforts.

Time Management and Productivity: On a global scale, effective time management and productivity are critical. World leaders and organizations can maximize their efficiency in addressing global problems and achieving collective goals.

Digital Age Success: As the world becomes increasingly interconnected through technology and information, the principles related to technology and information warfare and cyber security have direct applications at a global level. Nations and international bodies must protect their digital infrastructure and utilize technology for positive global advancements.

Economic Strategies and Wealth Distribution: Economic principles can be applied to address global economic inequality and poverty. Strategies for economic development and resource allocation are essential for creating a more equitable global society.

Adaptability in the Face of Global Challenges: The principle of adaptability is particularly relevant in the global context. Nations must adapt to emerging threats, such as environmental changes and evolving security concerns, and embrace innovative solutions.

International Alliances and Collaboration: The book's focus on collaboration and win-win solutions is pertinent to the international community. Building alliances, fostering collaboration, and seeking solutions that benefit all parties are essential for addressing global issues effectively.

In summary, the principles outlined in "33 Life Success Tactics Rooted in the Principles of War" can be applied on a global scale to address the multifaceted challenges of our interconnected world. Whether it's promoting peace, addressing economic disparities, mitigating environmental crises, or embracing technology for progress, these principles offer a strategic framework for success in the global arena.